*All Things
Bright & Beautiful*

DESIGN IN BRITAIN
1830 to Today

All Things Bright & Beautiful

DESIGN IN BRITAIN
1830 to today

by FIONA MacCARTHY

UNIVERSITY OF TORONTO PRESS

First published in Canada and the United States by
University of Toronto Press, Toronto and Buffalo

© George Allen & Unwin Ltd 1972

ISBN 0-8020-1869-6
MICROFICHE 0-8020-0202-1

Printed in Great Britain

This book has been designed by Walter Bloor DFA(Lond)

CONTENTS

I

The Cole Group
1830-1860

HENRY Cole, an early Victorian civil servant of adequate talent and exceptional zeal, decided to design a teaset. This decision turned out to be a great deal more important than it sounds. It grew into a movement for reform, a great campaign for improved design in industry, which even now goes on.

Cole had a motto: 'Whatsoever thy hand findeth to do, do it with all thy might'. And since his hand was forever occupied with projects for improvements of a limitless variety—from re-organizing the Public Record Office, introducing Penny Postage and reforming Patent Laws to unifying railway gauges and constructing Grimsby docks—Cole was a busy and influential man. He was really a professional reformer. But, when young, he found time to take a course in water-colour painting under David Cox; his sketches were shown at the Royal Academy; and, as a result, he was always sympathetic, through his other enterprises, to the cause of art. In 1839, he commissioned William Wyon, a painter, to design the Penny Black; and in 1845, he asked Horsley to produce an illustration for a Christmas card. The Christmas card itself was a Henry Cole invention; and so, for that matter, was the adhesive stamp. His excursions into the reform of children's books, resulting in *Felix Summerly's Home Treasury*, gave him more chances to commission illustrations: Redgrave and Townsend and Mulready were employed. It is not at all surprising, with this artistic background and his contacts with the influential painters of the time, that Henry Cole decided to extend his reforms directly to design.

The Society of Arts was offering prizes for a tea service and for beer jugs designed for common use. Henry Cole decided to compete, and as usual, he put his whole heart and soul into his job. He went to the British Museum and consulted Greek earthenware 'for authority for handles'. He went to Stoke-on-Trent and spent three days at Minton's superintending the throwing, turning, modelling and moulding. He set out to show that 'elegant forms may be made not to cost more than inelegant ones'. His teaset, submitted under his Summerly pseudonym, won a silver medal. It was also a best-seller for Minton's. It gave Henry Cole the idea that 'an alliance between fine art and manufacture would promote public taste'.

Cole's scheme, of course, was easier in theory than in practice. Fine art and manufacture were extremely far apart. The level of design in industry was then appalling, for a number of reasons. Among them was the fact that the industrial revolution had destroyed the old craft traditions of honesty and quality; as factories replaced small individual workshops, products became shoddier and also more pretentious. As stamping replaced chasing, as moulding replaced cutting, as transfer printing took over from hand-painting, as weaving became mechanized, there was no concurrent advance in design: though mechanical weaving was.

welcomed (and quite rightly) as one of the splendid offerings made by genius at the shrine of utility, this was not to say that the end product was inspired. On the whole, machine products merely imitated earlier designs for production by hand. Standards were chaotic. An ally of Cole's looked around him sadly in 1847 and commented on the confusion of the scene. He said 'There is no general agreement in principles of tastes. Every one elects his own style of art . . . Some few take refuge in a liking for "pure Greek", and are rigidly "classical", others find safety in the "antique", others believe only in "Pugin", others lean upon imitations of modern Germans and some extol the Renaissance. We all agree only in being imitators.'

Cole and his friends were not the first to realize the shamingly low level of design for mass-production. As early as 1832, Sir Robert Peel (who made his own fortune with the spinning jenny) had blamed falling exports on incompetent designs: he told the House of Commons that although British products were technically excellent, pictorial designs were 'unfortunately not equally successful'. The fact of the matter was they did not sell. The remedy, according to Sir Robert Peel, was simple: build the National Gallery to instil a sense of design in the manufacturer and to elevate the public taste. He urged the Government to grant £30,000 to finance an art collection. Lord Ashley supported the motion with the comment that artists and mechanics and the industrious classes in general would thereby be enabled to spend their leisure hours in an atmosphere of beauty 'instead of resorting to alehouses, as at present'. Mr Hume, perhaps more pertinently, contrasted the efficiency of the school at Lyons, which trained specialist designers for the textile trade, with the fact that in the whole of Coventry 'only one man was at all proficient in forming designs for silks'.

In 1835, eleven years before Henry Cole's conscientious teaset won its prize, Mr Ewart's Select Committee had been formed 'to inquire into the best means of extending a knowledge of the arts and principles of design among the people (especially the manufacturing population) of the country'. It was mainly concerned with the inferiority of English products compared with French, and the extent to which industry in England depended on plagiarized foreign designs; it also considered the comparative states of art education in England and abroad. For almost a year, the Committee collected the opinions of artists, industrialists and spectators, including James Nasmyth, inventor of the steam hammer (who insisted incidentally on 'the entire reconcileability of elegance of form with bare utility'). The views of the experts were collected together into a depressing 350-page report which concluded that 'from the highest branches of poetical design down to the lowest connexion between design and manufactures, the Arts have received little encouragement in this country'. The witnesses stressed 'the want of instruction in design among our industrious population'. In a panic, a Normal School of Design was set up by the Board of Trade in London straight away, and by 1846, when Cole began campaigning, eleven outer Branch Schools received Government support.

In spite of this activity—committees, national galleries, a dozen far-flung schools intent on training in design—nothing much had happened to convince the manufacturers that industry in Britain had any need of art. This was Cole's first object: a practical alliance between the fine artist and the manufacturer. In 1847, he announced the formation of 'Summerly's Art Manufactures'. His principal idea was to revive 'the good old practice of connecting the best Art with familiar objects in daily use'. He was evidently thinking of the time, about a century before, when George Adams, the King's architect, designed pottery for Josiah Wedgwood, and John Flaxman, the sculptor, and other British artists were employed from time to time by the potteries in Staffordshire. With great enthusiasm, Cole rounded up a number of well-known painters and sculptors, Dyce and Herbert, John Bell, Richard Redgrave, Sir Richard Westmacott, and other academicians, to co-operate with the 'most eminent British manufacturers' to produce such things as vases, decanter stoppers, christening mugs, mustard pots, bread platters; bread knives with handles in the shape of Indian corn; a hall stand for hats, cloaks and umbrellas, with a looking-glass; a lamp; a letter-box and brush-box and an inkstand all combined.

In practice Henry Cole was not a revolutionary: the works of Felix Summerly were hardly epoch-making; to a very large extent, they were true products of their time with their craze for ingenuity, their urge to tell a story. Cole is less important as a visual innovator than as the first great propagandist for design. Long before Frank Pick and Gordon Russell, far in front of any government-supported Council of Industrial Design, Cole was infiltrating his artists into industry and trying very fervently to raise the public taste.

Summerly's Art Manufactures were apparently commercially successful. Although the project ended in 1850, when Cole became preoccupied with plans for the Great Exhibition, his collaborators in this practical attempt to promote design in industry stayed round him many years. The Cole group, which grew increasingly substantial, carried on the movement for reform in other ways, constantly aiming to provide 'the enjoyment of taste to the enormous and now all-powerful bourgeois class'. They themselves belonged to it. They were the establishment: pedagogic painters and sculptors and art critics, worldly artists, earnest clubmen. The Etching Club, for instance, with its friendly monthly meetings, was a Cole group social centre and recruiting gound as well.

This was the essential Cole group: John Bell, sculptor and designer for Summerly; William Dyce, painter and friend of the Nazarenes, for five years head of the School of Design; George Wallis, artist and pupil of Dyce, principal of schools at Manchester and Birmingham; John Callcott Horsley, a painter specializing in domestic and countryside scenes, designer of Cole's first Christmas card and teacher at the School of Design; Richard Redgrave, painter, Summerly designer and, once again, a teacher at the School of Design; Gottfried Semper, German architect, writer and educationalist, who first came to England for the Great Exhibition; Owen Jones, Welsh architect, lecturer and theorist; Matthew Digby Wyatt, writer and designer, Secretary to the Exhibition executive. This active and articulate and more or less creative body of reformers was later to include Ralph Nicholson Wornum, critic and journalist, whose outbursts against Cole were pacified completely by the diplomatic offer of a job as Cole's librarian. After taking office, his views were well in line.

Cole's group was very worthy, level-headed and efficient; moderate in outlook and methodical in practice. Reform of design entailed a sequence of committees, a series of reports and pressures on the Government. But curiously close to these well-disciplined endeavours loomed the unconventional figure of Augustus Welby Northmore Pugin, architect, Gothic revivalist, author, pamphleteer, the man who wore a sailor's suit to travel on commissions, the man who received visitors flamboyant in his breeches, with silk stockings and a velvet cloak and candlestick held high. Before he died of madness (after three wives and innumerable children) at the age of 40, Pugin had established his own art workshops, anticipating Morris and all the Arts and Crafts. He had also propounded theories which quite obviously basically influenced Henry Cole and friends: in *True Principles of Pointed or Christian Architecture*, published in 1841, he maintains that 'all beautiful forms in architecture are based on the soundest principles of utility'. And although his ideals were more extreme than Cole's, springing from his passionate Catholic conviction that mediaeval Gothic was the godliest of styles, the two were in basic agreement on the point that 'the great test of architectural beauty is the fitness of the design to the purpose for which it is intended'. So much so that Pugin, who was not a born committee man, sat on the judging panel to select exhibits from the 1851 display for Cole's new Museum of Ornamental Art.

The rational side of Pugin, his 'soundest principles', his emphasis on fitness for purpose and good sense, are evident in all the Cole group writings of the period. They dominate Cole's *Journal of Design and Manufactures*. For Cole, like many subsequent reformers, had decided that to publicize his movement he must have a magazine. The first volume was issued in March 1849. There were 'Forty-Four Fabric Patterns inserted and upwards of two hundred engravings'. There were contributions from Dyce and Owen Jones, Matthew Digby Wyatt and John Bell and a paper from the German Gottfried Semper, all battering away at design in British industry. Wrote the critics of 1849: 'The more we see of this subject the more satisfied we become that every one concerned with it—the public, manufacturers, designers, art workmen, and ourselves—have all very much indeed to learn.' (One has only to turn to critics writing in 1949, the year in which *Design* magazine was first produced, to see that this view of things survived almost unaltered, in spite of all attempts at reformation of design.)

The Journal, like Henry Cole himself, was multi-purpose. It was published ostensibly for British manufacturers: in fact it purported, at one time, to be their spokesman. It was, simultaneously, Henry Cole's weapon in a running battle with the Schools of Design and with the *Art Union Journal*; it publicized (and even sometimes criticized) Summerly's Art. It had the general function of disseminating principles of ornament, of laying down the law that decoration should consist of appropriate motifs drawn from nature, strictly related to the object's use. In general, it advertised the stylized, flat patterns which in the view of Cole—and Pugin long before him—had more moral validity than freer natural styles. Criticism of new products, always frank and often rude, help throughout the *Journal* to put Cole's ideas across. A trowel with amorini decoration is detested: 'we think it ought to be unmistakeably a trowel'.

The first of the Journals was dedicated to Prince Albert, President of the Society of Arts: 'In respectful acknowledgement of the uniform and successful endeavours of His Royal Highness to aid the progress of the arts and manufactures of His adopted country.' This grateful dedication was more than surface politeness. Henry Cole and Prince Albert by then worked hand in glove. The Cole group's basic catch-phrase, 'art applied to industry', was said to have originated with the Prince. For Prince Albert was deeply interested in design, both in theory and in practice. His theories derived from the virtuous criteria of his fellow-countrymen, the Nazarenes, with their near-religious sense of vocation and their emphasis on honest, earnest craftsmanship, of which the work of Semper is a perfect, dull example. The practice of Prince Albert—who designed a small variety of trophies and adornments, a royal billiard table and the Balmoral tartan (grey, black, lavender and red)—was not perhaps distinguished, but endearingly wholehearted. The details of all palace decorations much concerned him; in 1845, for instance, he was busy with samples of new wallpapers to smarten Osborne House.

He and Henry Cole had a great amount in common: a moral sense of beauty, an obsession for detail. Their first meeting was propitious. The Prince was searching out old furniture from Carlton House, which was said to have been stored in Carlton Terrace. Prince Albert duly found it in the former Riding School, along with George IV's collection of armour. He then discovered Cole, working in an outpost of the Public Record Office, a model of efficiency with neat and tidy storage and exemplary methods of classification, and even a small hand-press used for printing ticket-dockets. Such care and ingenuity could not pass unadmired. Cole's reputation was, later, boosted further when Prince Albert went to lay the cornerstone at Grimsby docks. The Prince was entertained en route by train with a collection of relevant books and maps and charts and drawings, arranged in his carriage by the ever-thoughtful Cole. There was even a Dürer print on the wall. The Prince was reported to be 'very much pleased'.

The Prince had a natural interest in promoting art in industry. From 1843, as President of the Society of Arts, he stressed the great need to encourage 'more efficiently the application of the Fine Arts to our manufactures' in order 'to wed high art with mechanical skill'. He encouraged the Society to organize a series of selective industrial design exhibitions, with medals for outstanding examples of the marriage of art and technique. It was one of these medals, in 1846, which Cole's 'Felix Summerly' teaset had won.

Between them, Prince Albert and bemedalled Henry Cole tried hard to resurrect the Society of Arts which had been founded in 1754 'for the encouragement of arts, manufactures and commerce', but which from the day of its foundation had proved fairly ineffective: it was almost moribund. The Prince and Cole agreed that strictly-chosen exhibitions of industrial design would raise the public taste and prove to manufacturers how art might be applied. The scheme was quite successful: attendance figures rose from 20,000 in 1847 to 100,000 in 1849. But Cole came under fire for the preponderance of Summerly Art Manufactures in the displays at the Society of Arts. Cole's autocratic methods were apparently resented; inevitably, maybe, he was known as 'Old King Cole'.

These small exhibitions gave way to an immense one: the Great Exhibition of 1851. Who was the progenitor, Prince Albert or King Cole? Both were so involved in it that this is not quite clear. But Cole is on record as proposing to Prince Albert, in January 1848, a series of national industrial design exhibitions; Prince Albert sounded out some members of the cabinet and though, at this juncture, they were unenthusiastic, Cole's original suggestion no doubt paved the way for the Great Exhibition. There were long negotiations. Cole and Digby Wyatt went to canvass manufacturers and Cole, a little recklessly, hinted that Prince Albert was behind the exhibition scheme; this got him into trouble. Cole and Digby Wyatt also went to Paris to report on the French industrial exhibition of 1849. The London exhibition, to Prince Albert's greater glory, had by then become more or less a certainty.

Cole was on the planning committee, and was later granted leave of absence from the Public Record Office to serve on the Exhibition executive. He and his friends from the Art Manufactures and the *Journal of Design* were fully occupied with the Great Exhibition, making plans and making comments. They were jubilant. The *Journal of Design* rejoiced at the impending improvement in the standards of industrial products. Matthew Digby Wyatt expected Paxton's building to exercise a powerful influence on national tastes. All in all, a very splendid day of judgement was foreseen: in the words of a Cole spokesman, 'Since the period of the Reformation we believe the prospects of Design have never been so good as at the present time in England.' Prince Albert's prophecies were still more optimistic: praising 'the great principle of division of labour' and 'the stimulus of competition and capital', he came to a crescendo, 'So man is approaching a more complete fulfilment of that great and sacred mission he has to perform in this world.'

After this, the Exhibition was a fearful anti-climax. Queen Victoria liked it; but Queen Victoria would. Her comment that '*Such* efforts have been made, and our people have shown *such* taste in their manufactures' cut very little ice with Cole and his stern council of industrial design. The Queen 'felt so grateful to the great God', but the critics hit out at the tasteless manufacturers, condemning all objects offending against the principle of appropriate ornament. There were thousands: from blatant absurdities like the notorious Town Mansion House for bees to humbler iniquities like carpets filled with holes, wallpapers showing landscape in perspective, slabs of glass made to imitate marble, pieces of metal textured as chain-mail, creations in grass and dyed flowers and chocolate, beautiless contraptions of extreme complexity, in general — according to an irate spectator — 'startling novelty or meretricious decoration leading, in most cases, to an extreme redundancy of ornament'. Past styles, in all directions, underwent most gross revivals; Owen Jones, irritated and astounded, deprecated 'the vain and foolish attempt to make the art which faithfully represents the wants, the faculties and the feelings of one people, represent those of another people under totally different conditions'.

Owen Jones found the Great Exhibition most dispiriting: it proved that we were far behind our European neighbours; it showed that we were plunged in 'chaos and disorder in art'; it revealed the manufacturers' incredible stupidity: 'We are amazed at the shortsightedness of the manufacturers, who do not see how much it would be in their interest to begin by having a real and proper design from the hands of an artist.' Shortsighted manufacturers: this charge was to be levelled again and again by reformers of design. The artistic vicious circle which Jones described so forcefully recurs, of course, in every subsequent design campaign: 'No improvement can take place in the art of the present generation until all classes, artists, manufacturers, and the public are better educated in art, and the existence of general principles is more generally recognized.' Jones' plans for education involved the installation of an art museum in every town and a drawing-school in every village. Education by example was a basic Cole group creed.

For they speak with one voice, Cole and Jones, Semper and Wyatt, self-confident and reasonable, intelligent and crisp. Redgrave's *Supplementary Report on Design in the Great Exhibition* is typically sensible. His comments on the constant lack of fitness lead quite neatly into a Cole group lesson on design: for china and glass 'the purest forms should be sought, allied to the greatest convenience and capaciousness; and the requisite means of lifting, holding, supporting—of filling, emptying and cleansing, should engage the attention of the designer, before the subject of their ornamentation is at all entered upon'. He argues for the technical education of the designer, insisting that schools should contain workshops 'where the specialities of design may be fully explained'. He also recommends the employment of designers on an executive level in the firm. This long before the Bauhaus, a century ahead of the drive for Design Management: surprisingly advanced.

In fact the aesthetic criteria of the Cole group were those of the *Architectural Review* circa 1930. The objects which they tolerated are the products with no claim to beauty whatsoever: the functional machinery, the humble cooking stove, the invalid chair with its unpretentious structure. Gottfried Semper commented that, in the Exhibition, only 'objects in which the seriousness of their use does not allow for anything unnecessary, e.g. coaches, weapons, musical instruments and the like, sometimes showed a higher degree of soundness in decoration and in the methods by which the value of functionally defined forms is enhanced'. Wyatt, in the *Journal of Design*, wrote most ecstatically on the wonders of the Menai and the Conway iron bridges.

When the Exhibition ended, the Cole group was constructive. They had obviously decided to salvage what they could and to channel the £186,000 profit from the Exhibition towards 'the promotion of science and art and their applications in productive industry', trying to ensure that the 6 million people who contentedly thronged the Crystal Palace could be made to change their tastes. On Prince Albert's advice, and no doubt with Cole's approval, the Commissioners bought 87 acres at South Kensington for building an educational complex of museums and colleges. Wyatt finally judged the Exhibition an 'extraordinary stimulant', which could awaken all their energies: 'men's minds', he announced 'are now earnestly directed to the subject of restoring to symmetry all that had fallen into disorder.'

Henry Cole, who was of course the most symmetrical of men, was busily spending £5,000 on the most instructive exhibits he could salvage from the Crystal Palace for his own Museum of Manufactures. Agreeing with Semper that 'Public monuments and collections are the true teachers of a free people', a committee consisting of Cole, Herbert, Redgrave, Owen Jones and Pugin selected Elkington electrotypes, china from Minton and Sevres, oriental arms and armour, Belgian gold and silver, and other striking objects, including—perhaps from politeness—a few of Pugin's chalices. To this well-intentioned collection were added all the samples which had been kept in lamentable disarray at the Schools of Design, and objects which were bought from the 1844 Exhibition in Paris. Cole sifted them all through and set up his Museum of Manufactures in Marlborough House.

It was mainly for the benefit of students; but the public keenly attended the museum exhibitions. Prince Albert liked the scheme and gave Henry Cole permission to search the Palace cupboards for examples of Sevres china. The British manufacturers were less enthusiastic when Cole set up a Chamber of Horrors in design, naming the producers. Charles Dickens, to whom Cole was anathema, makes use of the Museum for the scene in *Household Words* in which Mr Crumpet of Clump Lodge in Brixton returns home discontented with his own design for living and is terribly haunted 'by horrible shapes'. Needless to say, such was the outcry that Cole's pedantic horrors were very soon dispersed. The Museum, renamed more grandly the Museum of Ornamental Art, later moved to South Kensington and later still became the Victoria and Albert. It is more of a monument, in fact, to Henry Cole.

Alongside the Museum, Cole was now in charge of the School of Design. He had been eyeing it for years. For Cole could not resist the call for reformation, and the School of Design had been an out-and-out fiasco. Already, two government committees had examined the failure of the institution, concluding wanly that 'there has been an immensity of time consumed in disputations on modes of instruction and management, that might have been far more beneficially devoted to the practical business of the School'. Already Henry Cole, requested to write an official report on improvements for the school, had untiringly produced not one report but three, recording the growing dissatisfaction of manufacturers. Cole sympathized, of course, with the industrialists' view.

The trouble was that no one, in the main school or the Branch schools, knew how to set about a training for design. They could not decide whether students should be given a broad training in art, including life drawing, or whether the course should be commercial and technical, with industrial machinery instead of human figures. The argument for nose-to-the-grindstone design training was forcefully expressed by Gabriel Tinto who claimed that

'The moment the artisan student is taught to be an artist instead of a draughtsman, his mind becomes unsettled and aspirations arise in his bosom calculated to lead him out of the sure and solid path of commerce into the thorny and devious tract which leads to Fine Art.'

When, in Manchester, a nude female model had a fit in a corridor, life drawing was banned for fourteen years.

Characteristically, Cole was well set on the sure and solid path of commerce. He believed that students should be trained to be of immediate use to industry: none of this high art, but a practical course in geometry and ornamental copying. 'This is the beginning of the end,' said the *Art Journal* at the news of his appointment. But Cole was quite impervious to rudeness. He was, luckily for him, utterly self-confident. Installed as Superintendent of the Department of Practical Art, with Richard Redgrave as Art-Superintendent in charge of the London School, he sat back and pronounced, with benign smugness,

'We cannot hope to escape from mistakes, but we trust that vigilance, firmness, prudence and conciliation, will reduce the number and afford a fair trial in this new attempt to afford practical art instruction.'

Systematically, Cole set off on a tour of Europe: Berlin, Dresden and Vienna. Systematically, he aimed to reorganize entirely national art training, to strengthen the school in London in its role as provider of designers for industry and teachers for the board schools, to establish a network of practical, and self-supporting, art schools in the provinces. He emphasized the need for national drawing classes, for he believed that 'the improvement of manufactures is altogether dependent upon the public sense of the necessity of it, and the public ability to judge between what is good and bad in art'. By 1864, at the time of another Select Committee, Cole's achievements were impressive: 90 art schools with 16,000 students; art teachers teaching 70,000 schoolchildren. On paper, Cole was excellent at making systems work.

But in practice his success was limited. His products, the Summerly Art Manufactures, made no lasting impact. His promotional activities got him almost nowhere: by 1874, a series of industrial design exhibitions had to be curtailed for lack of support. What is more, his friends and pupils, in terms of actual products, made little contribution to the progress of design. George Moore maintained: 'The schools were primarily intended as schools of design where the sons and the daughters of the people would be taught how to design wallpapers.' The attack is very waspish, but pretty nearly true.

The only designer of Cole's generation to work with manufacturers consistently and practically was Alfred Stevens, a sculptor outside Cole's group, with reactionary Italianate-academic views. The only designer of successive generations to work industrially with any genius was Dresser: Christopher Dresser, Doctor of Botany and lecturer on principles of ornamentation, on whom (so they said) Owen Jones' mantle seemed to have fallen. But he did not let it swamp him. He travelled to Japan, and returned to pursue a career of greater enterprise, working three-dimensionally in pottery and glass and metalware, and opening a shop in New Bond Street. At Dresser's Art Furniture Alliance the attendants were 'robed in many aesthetic costumes of the period in demure art colours'. This 'added a certain air to the place': an air which, one suspects, Cole could not tolerate.

For this was 1880 or so. By then, John Ruskin had spent a quarter-century attacking Henry Cole. Ruskin's swarthy Christianity, his love of natural nature and his overall idealism cried out against Cole's pompous and bleak commercial outlook, the Cole group's flat, prim patterns, Cole's systematic training for designers at South Kensington. 'Try first to manufacture a Raphael,' thundered Ruskin, 'then let Raphael direct your manufacture.' And in fellowship with Ruskin, and quite opposed to Cole, a new reforming movement, both gentler and more rugged, more romantic, more humanitarian, had begun. Cole's tight neat attempt to promote 'an alliance between fine art and manufacture' was swept away completely by the larger proposition, more practical and also a good deal more fantastic, that 'the beginning of art is in getting our country clean and our people beautiful'.

1
Henry Cole
Teapot made by Summerly's Art
Manufactures, 1846.

2
Christopher Dresser
Silver-mounted decanter and glasses,
made by Hukin & Heath, 1881–2.

I

3

4

5

3
Edward William Godwin
Ebonized oak side table made by
William Watt, about 1867.

4
Henry Cole
Teaset made by Summerly's Art
Manufactures, 1846.

5
Edward William Godwin
Ebonized oak chair made by
William Watt, about 1875.

6
William Burges
Painted cabinet, 1858.

6

7

8

7
Christopher Dresser
Silver-plated teapot made by
James Dixon, about 1880.

8
Bruce J. Talbert
'Hatton' silk damask made by
Warner, about 1880.

9
Christopher Dresser
'Clutha' glass vases made by
James Couper, about 1880.

10
Owen Jones
'Athens' silk damask made by
Warner, about 1870.

9

11

11
Richard Redgrave
Water decanter made by Summerly's
Art Manufactures, 1847

12
William Burges (?)
Painted bookcase, about 1860.

13
Edward William Godwin
Ebonized oak table made by
William Watt, 1867.

14
Edward William Godwin
Ebonized wood sideboard made by
William Watt, 1867.

13

14

15

16

17

15
Owen Jones
Silk tissue made by Warner, 1870–80.

16
Owen Jones
Silk tissue made by Warner, about 1870.

17
Alfred Stevens
Door-knocker, about 1865.

18
Bruce J. Talbert
'Kingfisher' silk damask made by Warner, about 1880.

18

2

The Arts and Crafts 1860-1915

WILLIAM Holman Hunt, long before he painted 'Little Nell and her Grandfather', 'The Light of the World' or 'Isabella and the Pot of Basil', had down-to-earth experience of industrial design. He had worked as a juvenile pattern designer, from the age of fourteen, in Richard Cobden's London office, producing commercial designs for cotton prints. This monotonous apprenticeship influenced his attitude for ever; it gave him a passion for reform. He explained: 'My past experience in pattern designing and my criticisms upon the base and vulgar forms and incoherent forms in contemporary furniture, to which I drew Rossetti's attention on his first visit to me, encouraged visions of reform in these particulars, and we speculated on improvement in all household objects, furniture, fabrics and other interior decorations.'

Holman Hunt could find no furniture to buy, so he designed some. He started work, it seems, in about 1855. When he showed his 'small group of household joys' to his brother Pre-Raphaelites, 'the contagion spread', and soon they were designing and painting, sometimes making, new artistic furniture for themselves and friends. For instance: Ford Madox Brown designed a chair inspired by the Egyptians and a series of countrified ladder-backs, rush-seated and stained green; Burne-Jones painted a piano with a 'chant d'amour', surmounting a picture of female musicians and death; Rossetti painted stories from Dante, and Sir Galahad, on a high-back settle for the rooms in Red Lion Square which Burne-Jones and Morris had taken over from him in 1856. At this stage their design work was all quite dilettante, a high-flown kind of hobby, done in camaraderie. A letter from Rossetti, on the move to Red Lion Square, stresses the high spirits: 'Morris is rather doing the magnificent there and is having some intensely mediaeval furniture made—tables and chairs like incubi and succubi. He and I have painted the back of a chair with figures and inscriptions in gules and vert and azure, and we are all three going to cover a cabinet with pictures.' He describes the large round table, 'as firm, and as heavy, as a rock'.

One may ask what this impulsive, very individual feeling for reforming household objects has to do with the improvement of design for British industry. The answer is, directly, very little. Unlike Cole, who from the first was concerned with British trade and the economic consequences of inept design, the Pre-Raphaelites and Morris and the Arts and Crafts designers on the whole were rather ignorant of commerce. Some were even hostile to it. Most of them cared more for the quality of life, for a 'standard of goodness', than for national trade figures. In one sense, their reforms were much less practical than Cole's. In another sense, of course, their reforms were ten times more so. It does seem fairly obvious that without William Morris and Lethaby and Gimson and others of their kind, setting a tradition of designers in small workshops, establishing a cult of straightforwardness and soundness, truth to materials, attention to detail, that British industrial design, as we now know it, could never have developed as it has. There is a direct link from the British Arts and Crafts men, through the Design and Industries Association (which was in fact an offshoot of the Arts and Crafts Societies), right on to the Council of Industrial Design.

In the Arts and Crafts movement, Morris is the central figure. It is almost true to say that he was the originator. Once Morris was married and had moved from Red Lion Square to his new Red House at Bexley Heath in Kent, the idea came to him of beginning 'a manufactory of all things necessary for the decoration of a house'. Philip Webb, his friend and architect, had already designed stained-glass windows for churches; and so, wrote Burne-Jones, 'the idea grew of putting our experiences together for the service of the public'. In 1861, Morris, Marshall, Faulkner & Co. brought out its first prospectus, stressing the need for 'artists of reputation' to devote their time to decorative art. The early results were on view the next year, at the 1862 International Exhibition; the Morris firm showed, among other things, a sofa by Rossetti, an iron bedstead, sideboard and washstand by Webb, a collection of tiles painted by Rossetti, Burne-Jones, Webb and Morris, a pair of copper candlesticks too heavy to carry (according to Rossetti) and a substantial range of furniture designed in the mediaeval idiom, 'of solid construction and joiner made'.

Morris, Marshall, Faulkner, Fine Art Workmen, were publicly protesting against the prevailing style of decoration: the ponderous and complex, bogus Second Empire fashion. Walter Crane, a Morris ally, maintained in retrospect that this practical protest 'represented in the main a revival of the mediaeval spirit (though not the letter) in design; a return to simplicity, to sincerity, to good materials and sound workmanship; to rich and suggestive surface decoration, and simple constructive forms'. It meant the simple black-framed old English Buckinghamshire elbow-chair instead of wavy-backed and curly-legged stuffed seating, French-polished and often unreliably constructed; it meant bordered Eastern rugs and fringed Axminster carpets on plain or stained boards or India matting instead of 'the stuffy planned carpets'. It recommended slender black wood or light brass curtain rods; plain white or green paint for interior woodwork; canopied settles, plain oaken boards and trestles and blue-and-white Nankin, Delft or Gres de Flandres to brighten the dresser. From Morris' workshops in Queen Square developed a sophisticated cult of everyday simplicity, intended to offset *objets d'art* of lustrous splendour, and unique palatial pieces of ornately-painted furniture. This became a powerful fashion among the cultured people. 'Soon,' says Crane, 'no home with any claim to decorative charm was felt to be complete without its vine and fig tree so to speak—from Queen Square.' Though Walter Crane was biased, this was partly true.

But there was more to Morris, of course, than vines and fig leaves, more than a new rarified rich style of decoration. For Morris had already, at Oxford with Burne-Jones, embarked upon a 'holy crusade against the age', the crusade against the tyranny of factory production which John Ruskin, the grand-master craftsman, had begun. As an undergraduate, Morris had been highly influenced by Ruskin and, in particular, by Ruskin's *Stones of Venice*, published 1851–53; the chapter on 'The Nature of Gothic,' Morris said, would 'be considered as one of the very few necessary and inevitable utterances of the century.' When he and his friends first read it, 'it seemed to point out a new road on which the world should travel': away from competitive capitalistic commerce to groups of men and maids working happily together, away from massive factories to individual workshops, from mechanized banalities to skilful craft and truth. Away from Academic convention in the arts to warmth and sincerity and Gothic spontaneity. Respect and affection for materials was essential to Ruskin's reformation, and to Morris's as well. Ruskin wrote, in *Stones of Venice*,

'The workman has not done his duty, and is not working on safe principles, unless he so far honours the materials in which he is working as to set himself to bring out their beauty, and to recommend and exalt, as far as he can, their peculiar qualities.'

Taking his doctrines to their logical conclusion—that designers should master practical techniques—Ruskin, in charge of the Oxford Museum, insisted on building a column himself. It had to be rebuilt by a professional bricklayer: Ruskin's experiment had not been a success. Morris, as technician, was a good deal more efficient. He was no doubt encouraged by the architect George Edmund Street whose office he joined briefly, first in Oxford, then in London, in the Pre-Raphaelite days at Red Lion Square. Street, a full-blown Gothicist, believing that an architect should also be conversant with the crafts, learned realistic ironwork, joinery and building; for one of his first houses, he even made the staircase. His ideal of the multi-skilled architect, and his practical energy in carrying it out, clearly affected Philip Webb and Morris who met in Street's office, and there made friends for ever. It was partly due to Street that Morris would be found with his arms dyed blue up to the elbows, in his vats; that before he began printing, he made a sheet of paper himself, out of fine white linen rags. Probably Street influenced his endless curiosity. Morris was always needing to do more. In a letter to Wardle of Leek, the printers of many of his chintzes, he admits this restlessness:

'I mean that I can never be contented with getting anything short of the best, and that I should always go on trying to improve our goods in all ways, and should consider anything that was only tolerable as a ladder to mount up to the next stage—that is, in fact, my life.'

A disciple, C. R. Ashbee, attributed the Arts and Crafts movement to the earnestness of the Pre-Raphaelite painters, the prophetic enthusiasm of Ruskin and the titanic energy of Morris. What he did not add, though it was in fact important, was that Morris' titanic energy was tempered by considerable realism. He could compromise. On the whole, his own designs were not produced by merry parties of men and maids showing pleasure in their work; nor were they available for all the world to buy them. Morris' productions were never for the poor. Failing an ideal society, he seemed able to make friends with, and take work from, the people he opposed, the advocates of commerce; designing the Green Dining Room for Henry Cole's Museum, acting as examiner in Henry Cole's new art school, and making the most of the South Kensington exhibits, which profoundly influenced the course of his design. Perhaps this was his strength. He was not a lone reformer, shouting out against the world; he was in the thick of it, with Burne-Jones on his left, romantic, insubstantial, and on his right the sane and solid, kindly Philip Webb.

This was a period of incredible activity in the decorative arts (as the friends of Morris termed them). It was a two-fold movement, with a lot of overlapping: the tendencies, on one hand, were the airy and symbolic, with Burne-Jones and Japonaiserie and Liberty and Beardsley; the urge was, on the other, for the soundly-made and practical. This trend was very well exemplified by Philip Webb. It was the Philip Webb school, the less fanciful designers, more anxious to avoid than to create an exhibition, who had profoundest influence on subsequent developments and indirectly much improved design in British industry.

'I never begin to be satisfied until my work looks common-place', said Philip Webb, developing Ruskin's rule of sound construction and honest work into a plea for a certain anonymity of style in household design. Philip Webb and William Morris, Norman Shaw and John D. Sedding, all at one time in Street's office, spread the principle of 'comely and workmanlike' building, the concept of pleasant modest living: in short, the decent home. Their concern took them backwards to form the Society for Protecting Ancient Buildings, and forward to advocate the garden city. According to a member, the 'Anti-Scrape' Society founded to protect the ancient, became 'a school of rational builders and modern building'. William Morris was the Secretary. Charles Eastlake's influential *Hints on Household Tastes*, published in 1868, encouraged a simple, clean and forthright style of living, with furniture in sturdy rustic style, hand-made by honest carpenters. For the next forty years these ideas, with variations, were carried through in practice by Mackmurdo, Frank Brangwyn, C. F. A. Voysey; by Ashbee, Baillie Scott, Wickham Jarvis, Walter Cave, Edgar Wood, and Lethaby and Gimson and the Barnsleys; and, almost more important, by a manufacturer and seller of furniture for bedrooms, Ambrose Heal.

In 1882, the Century Guild was founded by Arthur Heygate Mackmurdo, pupil of and traveller with Ruskin, devotee of Italy, a worldly and flamboyant personality, unlike the rather dogged English Arts and Crafts mainstream. He was half-way to being an 1880s aesthete. But his workshop and his Guild were, of course, pure Arts and Crafts. Like Morris's workshop and Pugin's still earlier, the Century Guild was established to design and produce household objects of a kind which were unobtainable elsewhere; it intended to restore building, decorations, glass-painting, pottery, woodcarving and metal to their right place beside painting and sculpture: in other words, to make them no longer trades but arts. Helping Mackmurdo, from the first, were Herbert Horne and Selwyn Image, who had for a while run concurrent careers as a curate and designer. But by 1882, the Church had had enough, and Image was dismissed from St Anne's in Soho and turned his attentions to Mackmurdo's Guild full-time. Other members, and associates, included Clement Heaton, specialist in cloisonné enamel; George Heywood Sumner, master of 'sgraffito', with which he decorated many churches, and stained glass; and William de Morgan, the potter and perfecter of lustre techniques and Persian blue-green glazes, an enthusiast who worked on almost undeterred when a fire in the kiln in his cellar burned his house down, and a visionary who stated, 'One obvious use of lustreware is its application to domes and towers, and to all parts of buildings that catch the level rays of the sun.' The work of the Guild, Mackmurdo's in particular shows brilliance, a great originality, almost eccentricity, both in use of pattern and in structural design. It seems to reach maturity in the much serener, more fastidious work of C. F. A. Voysey, a younger designer, not officially a member of the Century Guild, but connected all along.

In 1888, the Guild of Handicraft was founded by C. R. Ashbee, a broadly-cultured architect with socialist ideals. The Guild had its origins in the Ruskin Class which Ashbee, in time off from his office, organized at Toynbee Hall for three poor pupils. This developed into the School of Handicraft and, from there, the Guild. The aim was to draw in young journeymen and train them in design for their specific industry: for cabinetmaking, iron and coppersmithing, lithography, draughtsmanship, printing, house-painting, sign-writing and patternmaking. Meanwhile, workshops, run by guildsmen, would produce and sell professional handicrafts and help support the school. The system of co-partnership of workmen was evolved to counteract 'the unintelligent ocean of competitive industry'; it challenged 'a vast output of rotten, useless, sweated, cheap industries, and a vast growth of nerveless, characterless, underfed cheap men and women'. It aimed to establish a standard of goodness: goodness in work and goodness in life. In 1892, the Guild occupied a large, handsome building, Essex House in Mile End Road. In 1902, at the height of its idealism, family by family, the Guild moved in a body to a kind of promised land in Chipping Campden, Gloucestershire, where 150 men, women and children settled in cottages, kept their own pigs and dug their own allotments, acted comedies in winter, held swimming sports in summer, played in the foreman of the woodshop's splendid band, chased, engraved, enamelled, constructed honest furniture, made silver and jewellery of lovely reticence.

In 1890, Kenton & Co., a furniture workshop in Theobald's Road, was set up by Macartney and Blomfield, Colonel Mallet (a friend of Macartney's who 'had taste and knew people'), Gimson and Sidney Barnsley and Lethaby. Each of them contributed £100. Inspired, so they said, by what they had seen in Morris's shop window, they set to work producing their own designs in their own workshops with materials they had bought themselves. They were friends, as well as rivals, of Morris and Webb; Philip Webb was our 'particular prophet', said Lethaby. The fairness and the squareness of Webb's buildings and his furniture influenced the Kenton designers, then and later. For Kenton, which was never a very serious business, ended very amicably after two years. They enjoyed themselves greatly, Lethaby explains, 'making many pieces of furniture, selling some at little over cost price—nothing being included for design or for time expended by the proprietors': they finally drew lots for the remaining furniture, and went their separate and influential ways. Gimson and the Barnsleys went to workshops in the Cotswolds, developing a simple finely-detailed country style. Lethaby, in London, as the leading design teacher, and later as the father-figure of the DIA, promoted the same qualities: the measured and the modest, the soundly-made, the gentlemanly and the sociable.

Where there is a movement for reform, there are committees: even the Arts and Crafts meant many meetings. The St. George's Art Society, a small discussion group formed by pupils and former pupils of Norman Shaw, enlarged its membership to make The Art Workers' Guild in 1884. Meanwhile, a group of decorative designers, caught in a hurricane one January Tuesday in Lewis F. Day's house, had formed another group for discussion, meeting in rotation at members' homes or studios. This group, The Fifteen, under Lewis F. Day, included John D. Sedding and Walter Crane, who describes its 'happy if obscure life' over several years until it was absorbed by the Art Workers' Guild and the Arts and Crafts Exhibition Society in 1888. Crane points out that the craftsmen members came from very different backgrounds and used very different methods; but each aimed at 'a renaissance of the decorative arts which should act through and towards more humanized conditions for the workmen and employers' and, in this concern for society, 'there were few if any among them who would not readily have acknowledged Morris as their master'.

William Morris, at first, took no part at all in the Arts and Crafts Exhibition schemes; although he was in favour of the idea in theory, he had very little faith in its practical success. Certainly, its origins had not been very hopeful. It had in fact begun as a revolt against the Royal Academy system of exhibiting paintings; an angry splinter-group of artists, with the idea of holding their own exhibition, had written to the papers and met the leading crafts-men to explore the possibilities of collaboration. This project soon proved useless: all the painters wanted was reform of the Academy hanging committee. The craftsmen, quite disgusted, left the artists in a body, and W. A. S. Benson, the metalwork designer, organized a provisional committee to make plans for an independent Arts and Crafts exhibition. The New Gallery, which was then in reality only a few months old, was engaged for October 1, 1888. Walter Crane's introduction to the catalogue reminded the public—snidely but forgiveably—that art should be recognized in the humblest objects and materials and felt to be as valuable as 'more highly-rewarded pictorial skill'. The exhibition was enormously successful, in spite of William Morris' misgivings and Rossetti's dismay when he heard of the proposals: fastidious Rossetti was pleasantly surprised.

The Arts and Crafts Exhibition Society made a great impression with its first six exhibitions, in 1888, 1889, 1890, 1893, 1896 and 1899. The opening of the 1896 Exhibition was clouded, of course, by William Morris' death; but, said his admirers, 'it was a splendid moment for a hero to die'. The exhibition showed work of extra-ordinary quality and individuality. Craftsmen were making a name for themselves: for furniture, Barnsley, Lethaby, Cave; for textiles, Walter Crane, Lewis Day and Arthur Silver; for metal-work, Benson and Rathbone; for silver and jewellery, Ashbee, Henry Wilson, Nelson Dawson; for bookbinding, Cobden-Sanderson; for printing, Emery Walker; for glass, J. H. Powell of Whitefriars; for musical instruments, Arnold Dolmetsch; for a variety of wall papers and carpets and furniture, a mantelpiece, a clock-case and a lamp-post, Charles Annesley Voysey. His con-structions were considered 'at once the most restrained and the most novel in the Exhibition'. *The Studio* magazine wrote of Voysey: 'His vivid personality is one of the chief factors in modern design—one that cannot fail to have immense influence on the design of the coming century'. And, as it happened, *The Studio* was right.

In Arts and Crafts catalogues, and in *The Studio*, there is a strong sense of the spirit of the movement: its deeply-held convictions and its almost courtly tolerance, its spiritual sweetness and its hearty slaps-on-backs. 'I want us all to be friends,' said William

Morris 'all to be gentlemen, working for the common good, sharing duly the common stock of pleasure and refinement.' Perhaps it was not difficult. The most important craftsmen were gentlemen already: they had been to public schools and on to university. Most of them were naturally friendly and gregarious: they liked long country walks, and discussions by the fireside with a great stone jar of ale, and suppers out at Gatti's where the old Italian waiter, whom they always called Tricino, was perpetually smiling. A typical enterprise, high-principled and jolly, was *Beauty's Awakening*, an Art Workers' Guild Masque, presented at the Guildhall to the Lord Mayor and Aldermen. The craftsmen had worked hard: Walter Crane designed the Dragon, Lethaby the Throne, Nelson Dawson (metalworker) the Sword for Trueheart, A. S. Haynes the Dress for Bogus. R. Rathbone, the lightmaker, of course produced the Lamp. Selwyn Image, the ex-curate, intoned a formal prologue. The *mis-en-scene*, one hopes, was rather better than the verse.

'The fullness of communal life' was the whole purpose. It led Ashbee to sing catches with his guildsmen after supper; it caused Gimson, in his village, to direct the merrymaking, personally leading the 29th of May. These genial impulses were very much connected with the new enlightened Socialistic movement in the country: with the Fabians, Sidney Webb and Bernard Shaw and Granville Barker, Bishops Ingram and Gore, with their ideas for Church reform, the foundation of new schools like Abbotsholme and Bedales with an open-air philosophy and brother-loving motto 'Work of each for weal of all'. The Arts and Crafts were fighting for humanized conditions; Walter Crane describes 'the movement in art represented by William Morris and his colleagues as really part of a great movement of protest—a crusade against the purely commercial, industrial, and material tendencies of the day'. If this crusade appears a little ineffective, perhaps it was because the protestors were perfectionists. When Morris left the Socialist League to form the Hammersmith Socialist Society, Walter Crane designed the banner and Morris' daughter settled down to work it. This is not the attitude which wins the revolution.

What the Arts and Crafts achieved was less a total reformation than a bit of added prettiness, a fresh and simple style, a new appreciation of the objects round the house, and a sudden quite fanatical respect for craftsmen's handwork. Faithfully or more or less erratically following the guidance of Ashbee, Guilds of Handicraft rose up in Birmingham and Newlyn and places far afield: Bromsgrove, for instance, had its Guild of Metalworkers and Keswick its School of Industrial Art. The Guild up in Scotland moved guildsmen to Stirling, seeking (like Ashbee) the pure country life. The Guild down in Bristol opened a showroom for 30 craft members to sell their work collectively. Even in Manchester where, said *The Studio*, 'discouragements beset the pursuit of handicrafts', Walter Crane, after two years' propaganda, established a substantial Northern Art Workers' Guild.

The Royal School of Needlework, founded in 1872, commissioning designs from Morris, Burne-Jones, Crane, Selwyn Image and Alexander Fisher, stimulated stitching in the school and in the home. The Home Arts & Industries Association, founded in 1885 by Mrs Jebb, with Mackmurdo's backing, propagated the idea of everyman a craftsman, and a vision of fair women all with needles in their hands. The romance of cottage craftsmanship was to a large extent responsible for numerous small craft groups, some professional, some wholly unprofessional, which quickly came to life: The Leek Embroidery Society, directed by Mrs Thomas Wardle, which issued sewing patterns; the School of Art Woodcarving in Pelham Place in London; the Haslemere Peasant Industries, founded by Geoffrey Blount, a Wykehamist, in 1896; St. Edmundsbury Weavers from 1901 in Haslemere; the Women's Guild of Arts; and many dozens more. The range and the enthusiasm of these peripheral arts and crafts revivals can be gathered from displays by the Home Art & Industries Association which annually managed to fill the Albert Hall. Exhibits included, in 1894, the brass and copper repoussé work, perfected by the parishioners of Compton Greenfield, Bristol, 'under the able guidance' of the Rector. The next year, pride of place was given to arts and industries from the royal home at Sandringham: a log-stand wrought in iron by the Princess of Wales, a little heart-shaped table with polished poker-work which H.R.H. Duchess of York had executed.

On a more commercial level, art potteries were thriving: the Martin Brothers, Southall; Doulton's of Lambeth; Della Robbia at Birkenhead (directed by Harold Rathbone, a painter and pupil of Ford Madox Brown). Howson Taylor, Bernard Moore, Moorcroft and Pilkington's Lancastrian Pottery were all experimenting with artistic lustrous glazes. When Pilkington's exhibited in 1904 in London, showing new opalescent and crystalline effects, curdled, mottled, flocculent and clouded texture glazes, a critic reported with a tone of ecstasy:

'In a great room draped with white were vases, bowls, dishes and trays, resplendent in all the colour of the rainbow and glittering like precious stones.'

Beyond the shining lustres, home-made silver, palace poker-work, the fluttering enthusiasms of the arts and crafts, a solider, more lasting side-effect was now emerging: the reform of official teaching of design. In 1894, William Richard Lethaby ('Richards' to his friends, who were the basic Arts and Crafts men) became an adviser on art to the Technical Education Board of the London County Council. George Frampton, the sculptor, was appointed co-adviser, and when in 1896 the Central School was founded 'to encourage the industrial application of decorative art', Lethaby and Frampton were made joint principals. Frampton never put in an appearance. So Lethaby himself was in fact in full control, concentrating all his energies into propagating the level-headed 'doing is designing' school of thought. Sweeping aside the method of training pursued at South Kensington since Henry Cole was there—a method which reminded Lethaby of learning to swim in a thousand lessons without water—the Central School developed a practical curriculum of craft techniques and training in the right use of materials. 'Art, construction, architecture,' exclaimed Lethaby to Central School pupils 'they are all one. You must go upstairs and see how stained glass windows are made and books are bound and gilding done.' The staff he employed were highly-skilled craftsmen: for example, Douglas Cockerell for bookbinding, Catterson Smith for wallpaper and textiles. Even a reputable plumber was brought in. Lethaby himself taught leadwork, and encouraged Arts and Crafts perfectionism mixed with lack of pomp, kneeling on the carpet, unembarrassed, to admire the workmanship of a metal coat of arms. He needed to keep up morale; for at first the Central School was very badly housed in Morley Hall, a building abandoned by the YWCA. The roof in the conservatory leaked, on rainy days, so fearfully that students had to put umbrellas up to listen to Harley Ricardo's lectures on architecture. But they struggled through, and *The Studio* reported that the first exhibition of work by Central School students fully justified the expectations raised by the staff.

With Lethaby installed at the Central School, another very vocal Arts and Crafts protagonist was appointed to South Kensington. In 1898, much to his amazement, Walter Crane was offered the job of Principal of the Royal College of Art. Crane, who had already been Director of Design at the Manchester School of Art, accepted reluctantly. When he arrived, he found that 'The School was in rather a chaotic state. It had been chiefly run as a sort of mill in which to prepare art teachers and masters'. He much disliked the system of cut-and-dried certificates: to Crane's admittedly unacademic mind, the curriculum seemed terribly mechanical and lifeless. He seems to have tried quite hard to put it right, to make the methods flexible and to improve equipment. But he found, as others have found before and since, that 'One could not order a flower or a bit of drapery, or obtain any ordinary immediate studio requirement without a proper form duly signed and countersigned in the right red-tape department.' It was all too much for Crane. He got on badly with the staff; a fierce attack of 'flu 'left depressing effects'; the job, which had been offered on a part-time basis turned out to be full-time, and Walter Crane was longing to finish the scenes in the Masque he was writing for the Guildhall performance by the Art Workers' Guild. Besides, his own design practice was suffering. He resigned at the end of the year.

But the influence of Arts and Crafts philosophies on the training at the Royal College of Art was not to end with Walter Crane's resignation. In 1900, Lethaby himself became the First Professor of Design at the Royal College of Art, doubling the influence of his theories that 'Designing is not the abstract power exercised by a genius. It is simply the arranging how work shall be done.' Until 1911, Lethaby divided his time between the Central School and RCA; then he retired from the Central to concentrate on his South Kensington professorship. Beresford Pike, the Professor of Architecture, watched the progress of Design at closest quarters: he describes Lethaby 'disintegrating the creepers and parasites of form, weeds which had planted themselves at South Kensington and taken root . . . and supplanting them with the healthy seed of truth and directness of expression'.

It is very interesting, although not at all suprising, that the influence of Arts and Crafts ideas was strong in Europe long before it got to Kensington. The Arts and Crafts, as usual, were more honoured on the continent than they were in Britain, and better understood. Early in the 1880s, Crane points out that 'In Belgium particularly, the work of the newer School of English designers has awakened the greatest interest.' The Belgian, Van der Velde, exclaimed that 'it was spring' when the first of the Arts and Crafts arrived from England. By 1895, when Bing's shop L'Art Nouveau opened in Paris, England was acknowledged as the international harbinger: 'When English creations began to appear, a cry of delight sounded throughout Europe. Its echo can still be heard in every country.' For Art Nouveau in France, Jugendstil in Germany, Secessionstil in Austria, Stile Liberty in Italy and all the variations in Holland, Scandinavia and even Spain and Russia can to some extent be traced right back to Britain, back to Ruskin and to Morris, to their new intense perception, to their love of handicraft. At the end of the century, to Loos in Vienna, the centre of civilization was London.

Morris and Crane, Ashbee and Voysey, Baillie Scott and Mackintosh, the Glasgow architect, were the best-known, most-admired of the designers on the Continent. Their work was illustrated in the magazine *The Studio* which had a reverential foreign circulation; Peter Altenberg describes the arrival of a new issue in a cultivated household in Vienna as 'a kind of silently aesthetic celebration, after which the master of the house had scant hopes of the fulfilment of more profane desires'. The British designers were shown in the flesh in the small avant-garde continental exhibitions: La Libre Esthetique in Brussels, for instance, showed Morris and Ashbee and Voysey and Beardsley. They later exhibited in the larger international displays which multiplied and prospered at the turn of the century: Paris 1900, Glasgow 1901, Turin 1902. British designers even worked abroad. Mackintosh decorated a music room for Fritz Warndorfer in Vienna. Baillie Scott, with six other artists—the elite of the continental movement—was asked to design the Grand Duke of Hesse's Palace at Darmstadt, the centre of a whole community of artists in which every object in every house was to be designed, in every detail, by the owner. This enthusiastic project, so immaculate in principle, was attributed to the influence of 'The English art of furniture making, the theories of Morris, the actions of men like Ashbee and Baillie Scott, of the Belgian, H. van der Velde, the Japanizing tendency introduced by the house of L'Art Nouveau (S. Bing) of Paris': not forgetting the contribution of the Germans, who by then had developed ideas of their own.

The Germans sent Hermann Muthesius to England. From 1896 to 1903, Muthesius, an architect, was attached to the German embassy in London, for official research into English housing. Sir Robert Lorimer later described how Muthesius 'showed the greatest interest and keenness in the British Arts and Crafts Movement. He travelled all over the country, interviewed everyone, got the loan of designs and of photographs of work and every kind of information he could lay his hands on'. He reported back to Germany. In 1898, he gave first-hand impressions of Ashbee's Guild and School of Handicraft in the German magazine *Dekorative Kunst*, stressing Ashbee's preference for functional forms. In 1901, Muthesius published a book on English contemporary architecture; in 1904 and 1905, he brought out three illustrated volumes on modern English houses, emphasizing sanity and sound use of materials, the fundamental principles of English Arts and Crafts. Simultaneously, encouraged by Muthesius, large folios of drawings by Baillie Scott and Mackintosh were published in Germany. Already, the Germans' design appreciation, with determined application, was a step or two ahead. In 1901, *The Studio* had noted in German government circles and manufacturers 'a far-sighted alertness to the practical value of good design'; the German manufacturers seemed to be determined 'to wrest from British craftsmen and designers their initiative supremacy in the applied art campaign'.

Once Hermann Muthesius returned to the Fatherland, lecturing and publishing, the Germans worked still harder. Wrote Lorimer disgustedly (as if the Germans cheated) 'every help and encouragement was given to the teaching of design for technical purposes. The immediate result was that a great amount of "New Art" design was produced, worse than anything of the kind produced here. But—and this is the remarkable and interesting part— a few years before the war, the Germans had worked through this phase, and arrived at the production of simple straightforward designs'. It was in fact in 1905 in Dresden that the Deutsche Werkstätten exhibited Richard Riemerschmid's mass-production furniture, a style of furniture specifically developed 'from the spirit of the machine'. And it was 1907 when, urged on by Muthesius (then Superintendent of the Prussian Board of Trade for Schools of Arts and Crafts), German manufacturers, architects and artists and interested laymen formed the Deutscher Werkbund, which aimed at 'combining all efforts towards high quality in industrial work'.

Meanwhile, back in England, the Arts and Crafts proceeded straightforwardly and calmly. They went their own sweet way. The Arts and Crafts Exhibitions of 1903 and 1906 showed the usual fine selection of expensive hand-made furniture, a sound display of admirable craftsmanship in oak, an English walnut cabinet inlaid with pearl, a pulpit inlaid with ebony, a decorative carving in silver, gilt-bronze and gold, forming a Gothic overmantel, intended 'for a room in which armour is hung'. Walter Crane designed a mace; May Morris had embroidered 'a truly beautiful cushion'; Mr and Mrs Arthur Gaskin showed 'a dainty little group of hat-pins and lace-pins', some of them with precious stones at the head. *The Studio*, which felt that it had all been seen before, was moved in 1906 to complain: 'The arts and crafts in this exhibition, almost failing to contend for improvements in the practical necessities of domestic comfort, have taken very seriously the covers of the books we shall read, and jewellery that will be worn in the evening.'

The Arts and Crafts, one must remember, were never open-minded. They were insular. They kept to their safe and sound ideals of wholesomeness. They disliked the new and foreign; they distrusted the extremes. Early on, they had detested the room which Edward Godwin designed for Oscar Wilde; according to May Morris, it was 'needlessly spartan—there was a hair-shirt vigour about it, opposed to all geniality or prandial humours'. With much the same suspicion, designers from Glasgow— Mackintosh, McNair and the Macdonalds—were disparaged, underestimated and labelled 'Spooky School'. Art nouveau was called 'the squirm'. When 'the squirm' arrived in Britain, when exhibits from Paris 1900 were displayed at the Victoria and Albert, Lewis F. Day and Walter Crane were outraged and three most upright architects with Norman Shaw connections wrote a very cross and stuffy letter to *The Times*, maintaining that 'This work is neither right in principle nor does it evince a proper regard for the material employed.' The spirit of the letter, the Arts and Crafts resistance to what was regarded as excessive novelty, also caused the architects and craftsmen, when the time came, to turn a blind eye to the events in Germany.

This is not to say that the English Arts and Crafts men opposed design for industry in principle. In fact, most of them designed for machine production regularly: Morris, Crane, Mackmurdo, Lewis Day and Voysey; Benson and Silver exclusively so. But, one way or another, design for mass-production was not what they believed in; it was nowhere near their heart. The Society they formed in 1888 for promoting art in industry was never very earnest. This National Association for the Advancement of Art and its Application to Industry—'a somewhat large order', said Crane—held congresses in Liverpool and Edinburgh consisting in the main of purposeless chit-chat and civic entertainments. The society was doomed from the first, from the moment at the inaugural meeting when Edmund Gosse brought in statistics of trade and the cotton industry—'"Things," as Oscar Wilde said, who followed him, "which we do not want to hear about at all." '

19

19
Ambrose Heal
Unpolished oak cupboard, about
1905.

20
Ambrose Heal
Wardrobe in chestnut, 1900.

21
Ambrose Heal
Unpolished oak sideboard, 1906.

22
Ambrose Heal
Inlaid oak wardrobe designed for
the Paris Exhibition, 1900.

20

21

22

23

24

23
Ernest Gimson
Inlaid ebony cabinet, about 1910.

24
Sidney Barnsley
Oak dresser, about 1899.

25
Ernest Gimson
Daneway House, Sapperton,
interior, about 1910

26

27

28

29

30

26
Ernest Gimson
Circular table, about 1905.

27
Ernest Gimson
Ladderback chair in ash, about 1888.

28
Ernest Gimson
Polished steel firedog, about 1908–10.

29
Charles Rennie Mackintosh
Silver-plated cutlery made for
Ingram Street Tea-Rooms, Glasgow,
1901.

30
Charles Rennie Mackintosh
White painted armchair, 1902.

31

32

38

38
C. F. A. Voysey
Machine-turned brass teapot, about
1896.

39
C. F. A. Voysey
Oak writing desk made by
W. H. Tingey, 1896.

39

40
Philip Webb
Chimney-piece in Red House,
Bexley Heath, 1859.

41
Philip Webb and William Morris
Red House, Bexley Heath, interior,
1859.

42
R. Norman Shaw's office (?)
Oak chair with rush seat sold by
Morris & Co., about 1876.

43
William Morris
Sussex chair in ebonized beech made
by Morris & Co., about 1865.

44
Edward Burne-Jones
Painted wood upright piano made by
Priestly, about 1860.

40

41

42

43

44

45

46

45
William Morris
'Flower Pot' embroidered panel,
about 1880.

46
William Morris
'Cherwell' hand-block printed
velveteen, about 1885.

47
William Morris
'Brother Rabbit' hand-block printed
chintz, 1883.

48
William Morris
'Compton' wallpaper handprinted by
Jeffrey & Co. for Morris & Co.,
1896.

47

48

49

50

49
A. H. Mackmurdo
Oak writing desk, 1886.

50
A. H. Mackmurdo
Dining chair with fretwork back,
1881.

51
A. H. Mackmurdo
Printed cotton fabric made for
Century Guild, about 1882.

51

52

52
E. G. Punnett
Inlaid oak armchair made by
William Birch, 1901.

53
Liberty & Co.
'Thebes' stool in mahogany, 1884.

53

54

55

56

54
Philip Webb
Vases and glasses made by James
Powell, 1859.

55
M. H. Baillie Scott
Painted music cabinet made by
Guild of Handicraft for Palace of
Darmstadt, about 1898.

56
George Walton
Table glass made by James Powell,
1903.

57
M. H. Baillie Scott
Painted seat made by Guild of
Handicraft for Palace of Darmstadt,
about 1898.

57

58
C. R. Ashbee
Silver dish made by Guild of
Handicraft, 1900.

59
Della Robbia Pottery
Earthenware vase, late 19th Century.

60

60
C. R. Ashbee
Silver mustard pot and spoon, about
1900.

61
William de Morgan
'Peacock' dish, late 19th or early
20th Century.

61

62
W. A. S. Benson
Brass or copper lamp, about 1895.

63
W. R. Lethaby
Inlaid oak sideboard, about 1900.

64
M. H. Baillie Scott
Clock, about 1901.

65
Philip Webb
Oak table, about 1860.

62

63

64

65

66

67

66
Arthur Silver
Silver candlesticks, 1906–7.

67
Arthur Dixon
Coffee jugs in copper-covered metal
made by Birmingham Guild of
Handicraft, about 1895.

68
Alexander Knox
Silver jewel box, about 1900.

69
Arthur Dixon (?)
Silver jug with ebony handle made
by Birmingham Guild of Handicraft,
1898–9.

70
W. A. S. Benson
Silver-plated coffee and tea set, made
between 1895 and 1910.

71
Lewis F. Day
'Strongstry' printed cotton made by
Turnbull & Stockdale, late 19th
Century.

72
W. A. S. Benson and Heywood Sumner
'The Charm of Orpheus' mahogany
and beechwood music cabinet, 1889.

73
Thomas Jeckyll
Wrought-iron sunflower, 1876.

74
F. Steiner & Co.
Roller-printed cotton, 1903.

72

73

74

3

The D.I.A.
1915-1928

ONE Sunday morning in 1914, late in the summer, two men sat talking, sanely and convivially, in a garden on Chiswick Mall. One was Harold Stabler, the silversmith: the other, the owner of the garden, was the artist Ernest Jackson. It could have been an Arts and Crafts discussion. As it happened, this was the beginning of the DIA.

The Design and Industries Association, which intended 'to instil a new spirit of design into British industry', was almost an extension, the phoenix from the ashes, of the English Arts and Crafts. By 1912, the Arts and Crafts triennial exhibition had become not only aesthetically timid but, at the same time, a financial disaster, and a group of younger craftsmen urged the elders to take action, suggesting that the Arts and Crafts should rent a shop in Bond Street. This suggestion was rejected. But the discontent continued: of the rebels, Harold Stabler was the busiest and noisiest.

The question had been raised repeatedly for decades: what future for the Arts and Crafts? What use to modern man? Nearly twenty years before, in 1895, *The Studio* had rather sacriligeously commented that 'Mr Benson's lamps could be more influential on public taste than Mr Morris': meaning that the metalwork mass-produced by Benson was in a sense more valuable than the precious handwork, the tapestries, the bindings, the mosaic overmantels, which crowded exhibitions of the Arts and Crafts. Two years later, the campaign in *The Studio* was shriller: 'Is it,' they asked 'beyond the power of a body which numbers nearly every prominent architect, designer or craftsman to face the problem of beautiful yet economic furniture? Can they not institute a section devoted to designs with estimates of their cost attached? Is it unreasonable to suggest that they should offer diplomas of honour to those manufacturers who would submit cheap and comely furniture, well-decorated pottery for household use, dinner and tea services and the like, artistic but inexpensive table glass, low priced but satisfactory wall papers, cretonnes and carpets?'

Although this urgent challenge was never taken up—there were never any estimates of costs, still less diplomas for inexpensive tableware—there always were some members of the Arts and Crafts quite conscious of the need for a much broader-based improvement in design. In 1898, Ambrose Heal's first catalogue of Plain Oak Furniture appeared; in 1901, Lethaby, in Birmingham, urged sceptical industrialists to upgrade their design, insisting that 'A *quality* department in a *quality* business must bring reputation'—and usually profit. At this stage, much the strongest and most direct effect of Arts and Crafts on industry was obvious in printing: the private presses, Kelmscott, Doves, Pear Tree, Chiswick, Ashendene, and others, helped to transform standards in the printing trade in general. (Their influence on Germany, of course, was greater still). J. H. Mason's Imprint type, introduced in 1912 by the Monotype Corporation, was celebrated next year with the issue of the magazine *The Imprint*, in which Lethaby attributes the British renaissance in printing to Morris' and Walker's and Hornby's good example.

All this goes to show that within the Arts and Crafts there were people who could see a little further than their noses. Stabler and his colleagues objected to the fact that so much skill and energy was so much misdirected: everyday industrial products were appalling, while high-minded artist-craftsmen found it hard to sell their work. Stabler, Ambrose Heal and Cecil Brewer, Harry Peach, and other keen dissenters, made the journey to Cologne where the Werkbund Exhibition of 1914 showed what had been achieved by Muthesius' cajoling, by Government support for design, by the German campaign for public education 'by means of lectures, exhibitions, lantern slide displays, and other devices by which the attention of people of all classes could be arrested'. This had resulted in what then seemed to the British a modern spirit 'full of vitality and hope for the future', an absolute acceptance of mechanization with its mass-production disciplines and anonymity. This spirit was summed up, in Cologne, by two exhibits, the model modern factory designed by Walter Gropius; the forward-looking glass house designed by Bruno Taut. The DIA forefathers travelled back with great excitement, exchanging notes and samples and proposals through the summer. Cologne 1914 had given them great visions: here, up to a point, lay Britain's future in design.

It was with these visions that Stabler and Jackson sat roughing out their campaign to begin the DIA, a British equivalent of the Deutscher Werkbund which had by then been active seven years. A provisional committee of seven was appointed. First meetings were held, not entirely inappropriately, close to William Morris' old workshop in Queen Square. The August declaration of war meant added urgency: for imports from Germany and Austria had ceased, and the Board of Trade, in order to drum up British substitutes, promoted exhibitions of 'enemy products' notable for cheapness and shoddiness, quite obviously untouched by the hand—or the machine—of Deutscher Werkbund.

The DIA, fast-acting in all the best traditions of Henry Cole's design group, wrote a memorandum to Sir Herbert Llewellyn Smith, Permanent Secretary to the Board of Trade, telling him the German exhibitions were one-sided: would he give the Werkbund a good showing? So he did. He lent several members of staff to the committee of the DIA, who had by then collected a small body of supporters, 'like-minded men and women'. They combed the shops of London, and ransacked their own homes, for well-designed German and Austrian products. Harry Peach, a stalwart member who always had his pockets and his rucksacks stuffed with samples, lent a number of exhibits, including a collection of finely-printed German books and pamphlets. The exhibits were amassed at Goldsmiths' Hall in London in March 1915. The exhibition acted, of course, as a recruiting ground for British DIA. A public meeting in the Great Eastern Hotel was followed, in May, by a more formal inaugural meeting in the Abercorn Rooms, with Lord Aberconway in the chair. At the first count, DIA members numbered 199. They were half of them, at least, Arts and Crafts men (the Images, the Anning-Bells, the Bensons) or architects inclined, in the way of Street or Ruskin, to believe in craftsmanship.

The executive committee met weekly, through the bombing and the anti-aircraft guns, far into the night, in Cecil Brewer's office in Queen Square. It was a period of strenuous activity and great good-fellowship. The shaping of the DIA, formation of branches in Edinburgh and Manchester (with more to follow), the drafting of the rules and agreement on a creed—consistent but 'not too inelastic'—all took time. Hamilton Temple Smith, the designer of furniture and member of this very first committee, later listed his eight colleagues. His comments in themselves, so stout-hearted and so tender, exactly show the spirit of the early DIA.

John Marshall, a Marshall and Snelgrove director, was 'a man of deep religious and artistic sensibility—a "spoiled priest" or perhaps a "spoiled artist". He it was who introduced (among other innovations) the bold pen-lettering for showcards, price tickets and advertisements, which soon ceased to be exclusive to Marshall's. But although he made his influence felt in the business world it was certainly not his spiritual home. When he volunteered for war I felt that he did so with a sense of escape; the news of his death in battle in September 1917 came as a bereavement but, somehow, hardly as a surprise'.

Cecil Brewer, the architect and cousin of Heal, 'combined an austere intellectual scepticism with a puckish sense of humour and a fastidious devotion to beauty. Already an ailing man when the DIA was first mooted, and while bearing his full share of work in a busy architectural practice, he yet found time to throw himself unstintingly into the task of forming and guiding the new Association. In so far as it can be said to have been built to any one man's design I would say it was his . . . by August 1918 he had worn himself out, leaving the DIA in his lasting debt'.

W. R. Lethaby, architect, designer, ex-Principal of the Central School, Professor of Design at the Royal College of Art, seemed 'the elder statesman—or, more aptly, perhaps the godfather of the DIA. He had been preaching the essence of its gospel for years, and had become an almost legendary figure during his own lifetime. He took little part in committee work, but his advice and pen were always at our service, and looking back, it seems to me that his philosophy of life was the touchstone by which we continually tested the soundness of our own ideas'.

'Fred Burridge had succeeded Lethaby as Principal of the Central School of Arts and Crafts, and this fact threw into sharper emphasis the difference in their temperaments. Burridge was of the planning type, admirable at framing unambiguous rules, writing reports of meetings and drafting memoranda; and he had strong views about reforming the system of art education which were not shared by all his colleagues, least of all by Lethaby, who distrusted all systems, reformed or unreformed. But the DIA got the best that each man had to offer, and not the least of Burridge's contributions was a sort of Rabelaisian gusto.'

'Harold Stabler was not only a consummate artist and craftsman; he was also a man of wide vision and imaginative common sense. He came of Westmorland and yeoman stock and remained a countryman all his life; perhaps it was an inherited instinct for doing things in their right season that gave him his flair for producing the idea for a new activity at the psychological moment when it could be most effectively undertaken . . . it is only now that I find myself wondering, in retrospect, how many of our best ideas were *not* born in Stabler's fertile brain.'

'His friend Ernest Jackson was an artist first and last—observant, witty and detached: he brought a certain astringency into our discussions, which was invaluable in keeping enthusiasm within the bounds of what was practicable. How right he was! (and how I wished that he could sometimes have been wrong, bless him!).'

'If ever there was a man with fire in his belly that man was Harry Peach. His watchword was "quality work", and it governed all his varied activities. It was expressed in his "Dryad" products and in the numerous pamphlets he published upon handicrafts of all kinds. His first love had been printing, and I think it was never supplanted in his affections. He was an insatiable reader, and in spite of troublesome eyesight he seemed to find it possible to read every book on art and design, both English and foreign, as well as every magazine and pamphlet on those subjects. He travelled widely and kept himself abreast of all Continental developments in handicraft and industrial design. A sort of latter-day "Mr Valiant-for-Truth" he spent his life hitting out lustily and impersonally on all sides, and exchanging blow for blow without a trace of rancour. It might be said that Peach was the incarnation of the DIA militant, and certainly nobody influenced its course more strongly than he.'

And lastly there was Heal, shopkeeper par excellence, workshop-trained cabinet maker, the main link between the public and the artist-craftsmen, leading figure in improvements in design of furniture 'and of all that belongs to the furnishings of houses'. Ambrose Heal and his associates in Tottenham Court Road had made 'unswerving efforts to carry into everyday practice the DIA principles of Right Design and Right Making'. Incidentally, the DIA symbol was an Ambrose Heal design.

As Hamilton Temple Smith had pointed out, Lethaby's philosophy of life was the touchstone for DIA ideas: Lethaby's soundness and attention to detail, Lethaby's insistence that design has no mystique. It is 'simply the arranging how work shall be done'; it is 'just the appropriate shaping and finishing for the thing required'; it is nothing but 'well doing what needs doing': a work of art is 'first of all a well-made thing'. Lethaby's articles in *Imprint*'s first issue expressed this in forthright culinary terms: 'Art is not a special sauce applied to ordinary cooking; it is the cooking itself if it is good.' He chose his image nicely; it made its proper impact; for DIA members were modest *bon viveurs*.

'The products of industrial design have their own excellence.' wrote Lethaby for *Imprint*, in his essay *Art and Workmanship*; this excellence is 'good in a secondary order, shapely, smooth, strong, well-fitting, useful; in fact like a machine itself.' His view of industrial design as lesser craftsmanship—plain, without much character, but none the worse for that—was not the German view: there, machine-made products were whole-heartedly accepted, judged on their own merits. But it summed up very fairly the attitudes in Britain, the ideals of the DIA reformers, by and large. These were moderate ideals: is it sound and is it sober? Is it measured, is it modest; is it common sense? Are sideboards appropriate to our belongings? Are drawers and cupboards of a convenient size? Do washstands permit reasonable ablutions? In short, has the product good reason-for-being? Stamp out serendipity: 'For us,' cried the reformers, 'there is no content or peace of mind till the community of plain honest folk may buy at moderate prices commodities suited to their needs, and satisfying their sense of beauty.' At DIA meetings, the members were incited to clear the decks for action, for (mixing metaphors in the excitement of the moment) 'the tucket is sounding and somehow we must go into action or strike our colours.'

The question remained: how? The DIA was friendless: the dyed-in-the-wool craftsmen accused it of desertion; industry was hostile, and the public mainly ignorant. How was it to propagate the fairly novel theory of fitness for purpose in design for industry, the 'essential prerequisite without which any design for an article of common use was just silly'? How on earth was it to realize its ideal of the DIA-indoctrinated business man in his pleasant office, seeing to the proper housing of his workpeople in dignified factories, pleasantly equipped canteens and recreation rooms? For, as they remarked in 1916, the work on which the DIA reformers had embarked was ambitious and far-reaching: they took in the total environment; they realized that few national industries were outside their scope.

Practical as always, the DIA did not attempt to move heaven and earth immediately. It started fairly humbly, requesting loans or gifts of lantern slides 'illustrating good or (for contrast) bad design'. Members got together pamphlets, organized discussion meetings, lectured round the country, pushed and shoved and argued, brandishing the *DIA Journal* which in those days publicized 'fitness for purpose' with aplomb. Hoping that the public would eventually help the campaign by refusing to buy domestic articles which they could see to be ugly, the reformers set about exhibiting exemplary design. In 1915, the first DIA exhibition, 'Design and Workmanship in Printing', was held in the White-chapel Gallery, and later toured round Leicester, Leeds and Liverpool and Dublin, penetrating to South Africa. It showed great energy. The next year, in the Arts and Crafts Exhibition at Burlington House, the DIA—allocated one small room—showed pottery and textiles. Fabrics for West Africans, coloured very brightly to satisfy the natives, were acclaimed by *cognescenti*. On the other hand, the trade thought the exhibition dreadful: off-the-point and pretty tasteless. Who were these young crackpots to dictate to industry?

Stoke-on-Trent was in an uproar (an uproar which, in fact, lasted half-a-century and even now reverberates) because an outside body, and still worse a group from London, had dared to pass a verdict on the products of the potters. In Manchester, the textile manufacturers resisted the idea of selective exhibitions of design by totally ignoring the DIA's request for samples for display in the Manchester Art Gallery. The DIA had written to 60 textile firms, and only three replied. There was nothing for it, but for DIA contingents to travel round the factories to find their own exhibits. This was one of their great virtues: they were dogged and resilient. The trade would punch them viciously, and somehow they bounced back to carry on their programme: lecturing the Drapers Chamber of Trade on design and quality; encountering the potters on their own home ground in Stoke, a group 230 strong, to tell them that frankly, 'Expert craftsmanship does not go hand in hand with good design'. In 1919, the DIA intrepidly formed committees to persuade the manufacturers to produce articles in compliance with DIA aims. At the same time, a register of approved designs, 'efficiency-style' products, was brought into being. An earnest Exhibition of Household Things, designed of course 'primarily to serve their purpose', was held in 1920. Furniture and fittings, pottery and glass, hardware, brooms and brushes—the main preoccupations of the early DIA—were arrayed in eight neat rooms. A critique of every product, in the style of Henry Cole's *Journal of Design* of 1849, interspersed its praises with suggestions for improvement. Efficiency was everywhere apparent, and discretion.

'Art is indispensible in life, and therefore in education and work': this worthy pronouncement, so sweeping yet so moderate, sounds quite unmistakeably authentic DIA. In fact it occurs in a Ministry of Reconstruction pamphlet, *Art and Industry*. For once the war was over, there were signs that the campaign for improved design in industry was taken slightly seriously by the government and by industry itself. The Federation of British Industries formed its Industrial Art Committee in 1920: the Chairman was Charles Tennyson; the aim, which was well-meaning if vague, was 'to consider the question of industrial art in this country'. In effect, this at first meant attempting to bring the training at the Royal College of Art into line with industrial requirements. The deficiencies noted by the Commissioners in 1911—including lack of training in design for mass-production—which led them to contemplate the closure of the College, were nine or ten years later just as terrible, or worse.

Again in 1920, another institution for promotion of design, with Treasury support, began a new campaign, full of wishful thinking, to create a market for industrial designers. The British Institute of Industrial Art had, in fact, been in the air since 1914, when the Board of Trade and the Board of Education had combined to consider and approve the scheme. The war had postponed it. But in 1920 the Institute opened in a flurry of activity: a gallery in Knightsbridge was permanently occupied by Institute industrial art and handicrafts, while three temporary displays of modern products were held at the Victoria and Albert Museum. Clough Williams-Ellis, reviewing an Institute exhibition in *The Spectator*, pointed out how closely its standards and intentions resembled those of the DIA: 'Judging by the usual commercial products of British potteries, a missionary should certainly be sent into "Darkest Staffordshire" with the Institute's little exhibit of well designed and unpretentious chinaware.' The DIA approved of the Institute's Bureau of Information, under Major Longden; for a while they worked together, and perhaps, had all gone well, a national council for design might have emerged. But this is not what happened. With the slump, the public money granted to the Institute was soon withdrawn again, and although private subscriptions financed desultory activities, mainly exhibitions and design tours through the 'twenties, these were not in general a force to be reckoned with. The DIA was virtually on its own again.

It has to be remembered that the DIA was still very small, for all its energy, acutely short of money. Membership in 1916 was 292; it was only 602 by 1928. The mood of early meetings can be gathered from the General Discussion, reported in the *Journal* for 1918, on 'Memorandum to Ministry of Reconstruction and Proposed Memoranda to Government Departments on The State as Buyer.

'Mr Peach considered the Food posters particularly bad, but Mr Bayes defended the frieze of silhouettes at the recent War Exhibition at Burlington House as decorative and inspiring.'

'Mr Brewer said that though the things mentioned might be bad, the chief sins were to be found in the Government buildings; the Post Offices were glaring examples of inefficiency and discomfort.'

The chairman seems to have ended the discussion with the typical comment that the DIA must not be too drastic in its condemnation. For although the DIA connections with Morris and the Arts and Crafts were obvious, its methods were now closer to the Cole group: its discretion, its businesslike committees, its lucid memoranda. Instead of jars of ale, it drank tea in the Kardomah; instead of Gatti's suppers, it ate luncheon in the Kenilworth (2s 3d per person, gratuity included). A lot of the romance of the Arts and Crafts was over; the DIA had settled for a life of common sense, urging its designers to talk man-to-man to industry: in the interests of appeasement, never mention Art. Their founders, they insisted, 'were not dreamers in Jaeger sweaters, with blue eyes fixed on supra-mundane peaks'. Not at all: they were ordinary men with ordinary needs and ordinary talents, who practised what they preached.

Little by little, saner and saner, the DIA built up its membership and influence. It did its level best to break the vicious circle (bemoaned by Owen Jones and still as bad as ever) of maker-seller-buyer. The DIA could argue for reform from a position of relative authority; for now, for the first time, the reformers were themselves manufacturers and shopkeepers. They spoke with some experience, and were not shouted down. Manufacturers important in the movement in the 'twenties were Harry Peach, maker of Dryad cane and metalware; John Adams of Carter, Stabler, Adams, the Poole potters; in textiles, Frank Warner, James Morton of Morton Sundour and William Foxton of Foxton's; in printing, Harold Curwen of the Curwen Press and Francis Meynell, founder of the Nonesuch Press in 1923. (Meynell with Stanley Morison and Oliver Simon later formed the Double Crown Club, improving the standards of design in trade publishing, dining and discussing: a club within a club.) In furniture, Gordon Russell of Broadway—as the *DIA Journal* for 1927 commented—was 'carrying on, in both furniture and metalwork, the tradition of the greatest designer and maker of recent times, the late Ernest Gimson, whose modest retiring life in the Cotswolds made him neglected by his contemporaries, but whose influence has been felt on German and Austrian design and is beginning to be felt here'.

The most enterprising shopkeepers were Ambrose Heal in London and Crofton Gane in Bristol, a DIA convert of near-religious ardour. The most vital public servant, without doubt, was good Frank Pick, a DIA enthusiast of quite a different breed, a sober meticulous qualified solicitor who went into the railways and became a chief administrator, first of the London Underground

Railway and later the London Passenger Transport Board. Pick, from a conventionally cultured education, with a working knowledge of international art, before the DIA was born, commissioned Ernest Jackson and others to design him some posters for the Underground. He was one of the first 199 DIA members. As he advanced in status, he punctiliously turned the Underground (and later London Transport) into a travelling exhibition of design, commissioning new buildings, new posters right and left, new maps, a new typeface designed by Edward Johnstone for Underground publications and notices, a series of wall-tiles for stations from Stabler. In his range of influence, and his love for detail, Frank Pick was most important: his actions carried weight. Like Henry Cole before him, he was part of the establishment; he belonged to the Reform Club, he was known, he knew the ropes. His great respectability gave prestige, which was much needed, to the DIA campaign for improved standards of design. With support from Raymond Unwin (the town planner), Charles Tennyson (Deputy Director of the FBI), Sir Frank Warner (textile-magnate and Board of Trade Advisor, Vice-Chairman of the Empire Flax-Growing Commission), and Sir Lawrence Weaver (London Press Exchange director, an ebullient protagonist for DIA ideas), Frank Pick gave the DIA considerable substance. And, judging from events before and since, authority seems to be essential for progress in design.

The Cole Group had been statesmanlike and literate. The Arts and Crafts and Morris in particular were speechmakers and writers; the Glasgow School was not (which is probably one reason why Mackintosh and Walton were so badly underrated: they never had their say). The DIA was lucky that its speakers and its writers were professionally lucid, with amazing staying-power. The most vocal propagandists were Clough Williams-Ellis, the architect and author, who was in from the beginning; Noel Carrington, the publisher and editor of most of the DIA publications; John Gloag, fiery critic of design, who had been initiated at a DIA meeting in 1924 by designer Alfred Read, and who saw the light so strongly that he preached, just two years later: 'The "something safe to sell" spirit, as dangerously stupid and unconstructive as the red-hot air of communism, is the great enemy of industrial design.'

Efficiency-style had not quite superseded the missionary zeal, the old tub-thumping fervour. They somehow co-existed in the DIA in those days, when meetings, according to Carrington, were 'like a conventicle of some primitive sect'. The heathen manufacturer had still to be converted; the tucket was still sounding, the decks were still being cleared. The DIA was actively persuading its adherents to dedicate their lives to the cause of good design. Among them was John Waterer, designer of luggage, who after the first war adapted the slide-fastener (the 'zipper') from military to civilian use, and developed the whole concept of lightweight bags and cases, in new shapes and new colours. He was an enthusiast for art and woodwork and natural materials, and music was his heaven; he was also a technician, with practical knowledge of manufacturing. 'About this time,' he wrote, 'I became a member of the Design and Industries Association which I found to be imbued with the same spirit as myself. To my contacts with inspired, far-sighted manufacturers, shopkeepers and idealists, I owe much.'

At this stage, what exactly did the DIA approve of? What did the idealists, then and there, find tolerable? In the *Year Book* 1923–24, Edward Harland & Sons, of North Parade, Bradford, advertised 'Foxton fabrics, Poole pottery, Lygon stools, Dryad cane and metalwork, Rowley wood pictures. Simple furniture, soundly designed and well made of excellent materials'. They knew their readership. For this seems an accurate measure of average DIA taste in the twenties, which glorified plainness and stoutness and trueness, and loathed the pretentious, the lush and the sham. DIA idealists liked Heal's straightforward furniture, 'properly planned and thoroughly useful': his clean cottage cupboards, his bright painted chests, his comely elm dressers, his weathered oak tables. They liked Gordon Russell's sturdy Cotswold-craftsman products; they much admired the hand-block-printed fabrics of Miss Barron. Whitefriars glass and Blue Moorcroft Pottery and Cornish Ware were endlessly in favour, and Wedgwood's 'Honey Buff' underwent a Heal's revival, and was fervently promoted as setting 'standards of good taste'. By way of Crittalls' windows ('art and commerce come together'), Lanchester cars, the Rolls Royce, the Bristol plane, the largest accolade was given to the Underground which was—not surprisingly—'perhaps the outstanding example of Fitness for Purpose on a vast scale'.

DIA approval was virtuous and certain; it had the stamp of Stabler and his yeoman stock from Westmorland, and Peach, the cultured rambler in thick shoes with ruddy face. The DIA in practice was more countrified than mechanized; its standards were consistent and unadventurous. If DIA approval was wholesome and predictable, DIA distaste was equally hard-set. The DIA did not, on the whole, like coon music; 'barbarous patterns'; the ballet from Russia; the Omega workshop where, from 1913, Roger Fry, Duncan Grant and Vanessa Bell tried vaguely to make everyday products in a new and better way. In much the same spirit as the Arts and Crafts resistance to art nouveau, the 'Spooky School' and Continental Werkbunds, the DIA held out against exoticism, strangeness and mechanization carried to extremes. Developments at Weimar, where Gropius had founded the Bauhaus in 1919, made no impression; events in Scandinavia, the pottery and glass in Sweden, and Kaare Klint and his Copenhagen furniture, were noticed and admired but not assimilated; the Paris exhibition of 1925, with its international jazziness and cubism and fireworks, left the DIA quite cold. The DIA reformers were intent upon their target, their British clubman's vision of national improvement: looking straight ahead and preparing for the day 'when not 100 but 1000 members sit down to Dinner in a DIA hall with DIA service and furniture'.

The obvious result was that for about a decade the international modern movement did not come to Britain. In 1927, when the DIA assembled a country-craft display for the Leipzig exhibition, this was all too obvious. Even Harry Peach, who chose it, had a hard job to defend it:
'It is not very exciting as against what the modern schools abroad may offer, but it is something English, and like all English things, sane, good, with fine individual work which will hold its own against anything the others may produce.'
Minnie McLeish, who went to Leipzig, was much sharper: 'Broadly speaking, we do not understand this modern movement in design, and do not like it.'

For the moment, that was that. But here and there designers, Alfred Read for instance, were starting to push forward. Paul Nash designed some fabrics, and Marion Dorn some rugs; a painter, Francis Bacon, designed pseudo-Bauhaus furniture. In the Cotswolds, Gordon Russell, the follower of Gimson and hero of the craftsmen, began to change his tune. In Oxford Street, a Russian, Serge Chermayeff, was preparing the kind of exhibition which had not been seen before.

75 and 76
Ambrose Heal
Dresser in elm with black margins,
1914.

75

76

77

78

79

80

77
Ambrose Heal
Cottage furniture, 1918.

78
B. J. Fletcher (?)
Cane chair made by Dryad
Handicrafts, about 1920.

79
B. J. Fletcher (?)
Cane chair made by Dryad
Handicrafts, about 1920.

80
Gordon Russell
Cottage interior, 1928.

81
Gordon Russell
Cupboard in Cuban mahogany,
1925.

81

82
Gordon Russell
Chairs in English walnut, 1925.

83
Gordon Russell
Dressing table and mirror in English
oak, 1924.

84

84
Gordon Russell
Circular table in Cuban mahogany,
1925.
85
Gordon Russell
Wardrobe in cherry, 1925.

85

86

87

88

89

86
Edward Bawden
Fireplace tiles made by Carter,
Stabler, Adams, about 1924.

87
Minnie McLeish
Jacquard woven cotton damask,
about 1925.

88
Claud Lovat Fraser
Printed fabric made by Foxton,
about 1920.

89
Gregory Brown
Printed fabric made by Foxton,
about 1920.

90
Minnie McLeish
Roller-printed cotton made by
Foxton, 1929.

90

91

91
Omar Ramsden and Alwyn Carr
Silver cup and cover, 1916.

92
Gordon Russell
Gilded metal fruit dish and biscuit
boxes, 1928.

93
Harold Stabler
Silver porringer and inkstand;
Wakely and Wheeler: Silver biscuit
bowl and cover; about 1925.

94
Harold Stabler
Silver tea set, 1928.

92

93

94

95

95
Truda Adams
Earthenware fruit plate made by
Carter, Stabler, Adams, 1923.

96
Ashstead Pottery
Breakfast set with oatmeal glaze,
about 1925.

97
William Moorcroft
Tea set with dark blue glaze,
1913–14.

98
John Adams
Early morning tea set made by
Carter, Stabler, Adams, about 1925.

96

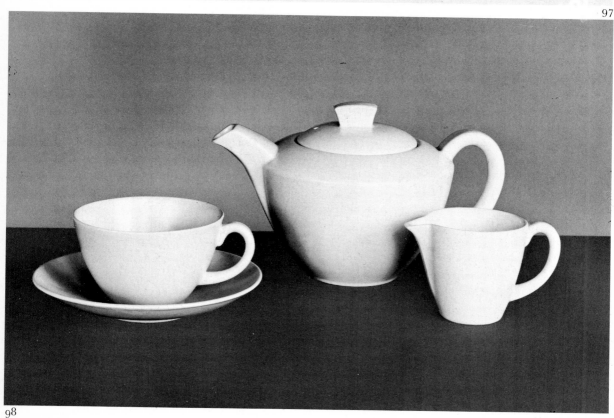

4

The Architects 1928-1940

SERGIUS Ivan Chermayeff, a Harrovian, an impecunious Russian emigre of greatest glamour, who had trained in art in Paris, married quite improbably—though no doubt quite astutely—into Waring and Gillow, the traditional furnishers. The wedding was in 1928. That same December, Chermayeff had cleared space through Waring's Jacobean furniture to mount an exhibition of modern French and English decoration. The salesmen were astounded, and so no doubt were Waring and Gillow's clientele. But the *Architectural Review*, which was in those days the harbinger of Britain's modern movement, was ecstatic, exclaiming powerfully (if naively in the circumstances), 'it really is inspiring to find great decorating firms like Waring and Gillow, whose roots are firmly founded in tradition, proving their right to be counted amongst the important influences of the twentieth century, by boldly declaring their faith in a modern point of view'. Among the *cognoscenti*, there was general agreement that Mr Chermayeff had excelled himself.

What he had done was to decorate a bathroom in red and black with curtains of American cloth, and to furnish a modern English home without a sign of cosiness or hand-craft or the country-cottage dream. Serge Chermayeff—bringing chromium-plated metal-tubing furniture and unit storage systems and rough grey stippled walls—introduced the style the DIA had long resisted. The DIA most valiantly tried to change its mind. Still upholding sanity, but altering its concept of what constituted sanity and what in fact was madness, the *DIA Journal* praised Chermayeff's 'sane clear outlook unencumbered by ideas and traditions that no longer have any meaning for those who wish to live an honest twentieth-century existence'. With quite surprising eagerness, the DIA admitted—or commented, at least, that it could not be denied—that Serge Chermayeff's interpretation of up-to-date furniture differed very greatly from the attitudes and methods of those whose creed was the teaching of Gimson and Barnsley. In the *DIA Journal* John C. Rogers pleaded for a national conversion, an ultimate rejection of the Arts and Crafts philosophy, arguing

'. . . it only needs an effort on our part to lay aside insular prejudices, to admit that perhaps, after all, our progress is not what we imagined, and we shall acknowledge that here, in Oxford Street, is by far the best thing yet done in this country to re-establish the domestic crafts and to fire English designers with a new enthusiasm. In many ways, the right note is struck, and given the support it justly deserves, popular interest will increase, and in a few years good modern design will sweep the country.'

He was over-optimistic. The reform was not so sudden: good modern design has yet to sweep the country. And even with such prodding, the DIA moved slowly: the stalwart old regime to some extent went on. The LCC report, published 1930, on handicrafts in

elementary schools resounded with the DIA doctrine of Right-Living and Right-Making and the charitable down-to-earth ideas of Harry Peach. The DIA kept up its hopeful old activities: its little exhibitions in Bristol and in Birmingham; its lists of Sensible Presents for Christmas (from Gordon Russell's showroom, from the Workshops for the Blind); its advertisements for Jolly Rag Rugs (hearth size, 3 guineas) and the Legion Book printed by the Curwen Press; its earnestness and heartiness, its friendliness and cosiness, its frequent insularity, its members' tours abroad. The report in 1930 of the Stockholm expedition goes some way to showing the DIA unchanged, from Frank Pick's disappointment with Stockholm Town Hall—the brickwork, he found, was 'rough and ill-laid'—to a DIA lady's poem on returning, which for full-blown camaraderie is surely hard to beat:
'A's Association, our noble DIA,
B the Briny ocean, o'er which we sailed away,
C—commodious Cabin, a perfect little Ritz,
D the Dining-salon where our figures went to bits.'
And yet, despite the jollity, the DIA had obviously not been to Waring & Gillow's in vain. The feeling among architects, Chermayeff and the others, that design was not a 'Honey Buff' teapot or cane chair but concerned with life itself, with creating whole environments, made a certain difference to the DIA. This was the period of the Cautionary Guides to cities—St Albans, Oxford, Carlisle—for which DIA reporters, out on day-trips with their Leicas, brought back frightful evidence of national destructiveness. This was the era of the petrol station outcry, when the DIA published *The Village Pump: A Guide to Better Garages*, and even the *Daily Express* was moved to hold a competition for petrol pump design. The *DIA Year Book* 1929–30 was entirely given over to 'The Face of the Land'. The campaign had enlarged itself: the movement for reform was becoming more imaginative and more diffuse.

At last, though for the moment in superior circles only, in Hampstead, in the Arts Club, in the architectural schools, the British modern movement, with fervent sweeping statements and socialistic principles, was underway. Unlike the mid-Victorians—Cole and all his works—this movement did not stop at uniting art and industry. Improvements in industrial design, when they occurred, were only the by-products of the wider, more ambitious, architectural activity which aimed to rationalize man's whole environment, with hard-headed large-scale planning and logical use of the most modern industrial techniques. Far away from Ruskin and the cult of heart-felt building, remote from the DIA statement ten years earlier that standardization was the last thing it should father, the modern movement architects, standardizing avidly, with quips about the Arts and Crafts and simple-life rusticity, set about creating a reasonable Britain. To start with, they suggested that men must live in flats.

Young architects, trained at the Architectural Association or under Professor Charles Reilly at Liverpool, stood waiting for commissions. But such were the conditions in Britain then, in slump-time, that commissions rarely came. So instead of waiting idle, a few of these young architects filled up their days with design for household products, embarking on schemes so rash and so unprofitable that they would not otherwise have seen the light of day. For instance, Robert Goodden, in a very idle office behind Blackwell's bookshop in Oxford, decided to break the monotony and design and market some wallpaper, called 'Asterisk': a great *success d'estime*. Another jobless architect, Keith Murray, filled up time, inspired by the Swedish exhibition in London, designing modern glassware and later on some pottery: Stevens & Williams and Wedgwood took him on. Keith Murray, who was virtually the first freelance designer for industry since Dresser, delighted the converted with his smooth thick useful glassware in smoke violet and green, his sensitive cut crystal, his matt-green Wedgwood bookends and tobacco jars, his plain good modern silver for Mappin & Webb. Pearl Adam wrote an article of praise in *The Observer*; Herbert Read picked out some beer-mugs in matt-straw glaze, by Wedgwood, as 'better than anything else in modern ceramics'. But in spite of all the glory, one-man shows at the Medici and displays from Lady Colefax, Keith Murray designed mainly to earn money to survive. He recollected eating with enormous gratitude a 6d lunch at an ABC cafe: a roll and butter 2d, fish and chips 4d, and a glass of water which, of course, was free.

It was partly economics and partly architecture which prompted Gordon Russell to change his course from craft-made, finely-detailed furniture to plainer mass-production. His younger brother Richard returned from four years training at the Architectural Association with the fashionable concept of bare, functional design for mechanized production and the broader social view of the architect's involvement with the whole environment. He altered the outlook in the Cotswolds quite considerably. Gordon Russell, in his autobiography, acknowledges the definite effect of Dick's return to Broadway: 'it gave us a link with architects and taught us to think in terms of rooms rather than individual pieces'. This was the position at Gordon Russell Limited, in theory wholly modern, in practice half-and-half, when the Wall Street crash removed a good proportion of the market for elaborate craft-furniture and expensive good antiques which the Russells had been selling to prosperous Americans. *Faute de mieux*, yet not unhappily, the Russells concentrated on lower-price furniture for serial production and evolved some most remarkable designs for Murphy Radio. These cabinets, machine-made, economic, yet presentable, were models of British design for a decade.

For the British were in many ways becoming more receptive. At last, advanced designers had taken to machinery. At last, the many goings-on abroad were not so suspect. Substantial foreign influence was suddenly apparent: influence from Denmark, where from 1927 the architects and craftsmen worked together to produce immaculate furniture, elegant and sensible; influence from Finland, where round 1929 Alvar Aalto designed furniture in laminated plywood (imported by Geoffrey Boumphrey of Finmar and by Findlater in Edinburgh, this soon became the rage at Fortnum & Mason, where the stools cost 7s.) Most of all, design in Sweden, its commonsense and modesty with bursts of great inventiveness in pottery and glass, affected Britain strongly when the Stockholm Exhibition and the London Exhibition of Swedish Art were on. The *Architectural Review* in 1930 gave over a whole issue to design in Sweden, and used Stockholm ammunition in its skirmishings with Harrods: if only Swedish standards were more evident in Knightsbridge, 'what a lovely shop Harrods would be'.

Temperamentally, the British and the Scandinavians were—and, by and large, still are—very much in tune: the history of design is one of constant interaction, backwards and forwards across the North Sea. But contact with the central modern movement in Europe, which was more extreme and tougher, was much harder to effect. In 1929, Jack Pritchard made a start by commissioning Le Corbusier to design—unlikely as it seems—an exhibition stand at the Building Trades Exhibition at Olympia for Venesta. Jack Pritchard, 'Plywood Pritchard', a young Venesta manager, an engineer-economist from Cambridge with great visions and a fair degree of impudence, worked hard to build up contacts with Gropius and the Bauhaus, the school which Gropius founded 'to exert a revitalizing influence on design' by providing 'a thorough practical, manual training in workshop activity engaged in production, coupled with'—most important—'a sound theoretical instruction in the laws of design'. In 1931, though Gropius had then left it, Jack Pritchard visited the Bauhaus in Dessau with Chermayeff and Wells Coates: the experience greatly moved him. Then Bauhaus work and attitudes quite soon infected England; wrote designer Clive Latimer, 'It was a revelation: here were logic and order, but also adventure'; progressive lighting companies soon turned out Bauhaus fittings; Gropius became a kind of household word. 'So great was our enthusiasm.' Robert Best, of Best & Lloyd and the DIA in Birmingham, wrote with admiration, 'that this name was even introduced into a DIA charade.' The DIA congenially acted out GROW PIOUS.

These were the elements which somehow came together in a good strong exhibition at Dorland Hall in London. It was 1933; the year that Wells Coates founded the MARS Group (for Modern Architectural Research); the year Berthold Lubetkin formed the

Tecton Group of architects and built the Highpoint Flats and rehoused the Zoo's gorillas. All this was important. For the Dorland Hall display was designed 'to give expression to a new type of civilization'. It was the result of a Board of Trade Committee on Art and Education under Lord Gorell: the 1932 report concluded (much as Peel had done a century before) that in order to raise national design standards, the citizen must be made design-conscious; he must be shown what constitutes a good design. The Report had strongly emphasized the need for exhibitions ('EXHIBITIONS mania', John Betjeman had called it) and Lord Gorell, the next year, wrote the foreword to the catalogue of the exhibition at Dorland Hall, which was privately sponsored and involved the DIA. With something of Prince Albert's paternal optimism and Gottfried Semper's theory that seeing is believing, Lord Gorell explained the exhibition was attempting to show the British public the best examples of the new industrial art.

What the public saw was a Minimum Flat, a Unit House, a large stone wall incised by Eric Gill with a joyful, frank and lustful scene of men and maidens, which the railway hotel in a northern seaside town had recently rejected, but which suited Dorland Hall. The mood there was permissive. The architect in charge, Oliver Hill, had given a free hand, in their individual sections, to Wells Coates, Serge Chermayeff and Raymond McGrath, and even the *Architectural Review* sounded a little overwhelmed by the results: both by the younger architects' talents and by the progress made by manufacturers, by Heal's and Gordon Russell, Carter Stabler Adams, Wedgwood, Dryad, Foxton and the Curwen Press which was showing wallpapers designed by Edward Bawden. The citizen, apparently, was pleasantly surprised. Bearing out the Gorell argument that selective exhibitions would improve the public powers of discrimination, a certain Mr Broadley (who afterwards wrote in to tell the DIA) went straight home to the suburbs to tour his local shops. He was quite surprised to find no Bawden papers there. 'I was saddened to discover,' he wrote glumly, 'that in hardly a single article displayed in any shop was there a trace of the Dorland House spirit.'

Remote as it might seem in the suburbs and the provinces, the British modern movement by then had spread just slightly. It had reached the Prince of Wales who himself designed a reading lamp for Easiwork, and rather in the manner of Prince Albert, maintained, 'There is always scope for new ideas, provided that the motto "Fitness for purpose" is born in mind, and no wildly exaggerated style is induced merely in order to cause a sensation.' This truly British sentiment was very often quoted. 'Design in Modern Life' had also reached the BBC which, in 1933, devoted programme after programme to the subject: Gordon Russell on 'The Living Room and Furniture', Francis Meynell on 'The Printed Word', A. B. Read on 'Light', Frank Pick on 'The

Street', Wells Coates on 'Dwellings', Elizabeth M. Denby on 'The Kitchen'. The list goes on and on. It went a bit too far for a listener in Southall who wrote to the *Radio Times*:

'I was relieved to find in your issue of the 23rd June that we had reached the last of the series of talks, "Design in Modern Life". We shall now be able to put the antimacassars back on the easy chairs and return our favourite vases to each end of the mantelpieces, and enjoy them with clear conscience as before.'

Signed, Two Old Fogeys.

It was obvious in 1933 and 1934, in small ways and in great, that art and industry were approaching one another: if not with arms outstretched, at least with some politeness. Cadbury commissioned designs for chocolate boxes from nine quite famous painters, including Laura Knight. Harrods, maybe nettled by comparisons with Sweden, promoted new designs which Foley's China had commissioned from 27 artists. (Laura Knight was there again.) Jack Beddington, at Shell-Mex and BP, with all the zest of a mediaeval patron, paid artists to design a succession of Shell posters. A magazine called 'Shelf Appeal' was founded to publicize activity in packaging; featuring (for instance) the work of Reco Capey at Yardley's and Norbert Dutton at Metal Box, where a new Packaging Advisory Service was actually charging for the work of its designers. Designing was becoming a kind of a profession. In 1930, after plans and counter-plans, meetings in Chelsea studios, committees in The Cock Tavern in Fleet Street, the Society of Industrial Artists was founded to serve two purposes which, its manifesto insisted, were of particular importance at the time: 'It is hoped in the first place to establish the profession of the Designer on a sounder basis by forming a controlling authority to advance and protect the interests of all engaged in the production of Design for Industry, Publishing and Advertising. The second purpose is to assemble the resources of Design as a vital factor in British Industry and so to assist the advancement of British Trade, both at home and abroad.' Five years later, a number of designers had collected, with more sophistication than was usual in Britain, to form a design agency, Industrial Design Partnership. Both of these establishments, Society and Parnership, were coaxed into being by Milner Gray, a quintessential diplomat and capable designer, a clubman and a wit, a Cole group man reborn. One of his new partners was a much more unknown quantity, a Russian and an expert in display-work: Misha Black.

Round this time there was a sudden profusion of modernistic exhibitions: 'Modern Architecture' at the new RIBA, 'Modern Silverware' at Goldsmiths' Hall, 'Modern Living' at Whiteley's, another Dorland Hall which seems to have turned out a comparative fiasco. (Wells Coates, Serge Chermayeff, Ambrose Heal, Maxwell Fry, Jack Pritchard and other angry men wrote com-

plaining of frivolity and far too many fashionable 'amusing' ideas.)
Round this time, there was a sudden pile of books about design:
Geoffrey Holme's *Industrial Design and the Future*, John Gloag's
Design in Modern Life and *Industrial Art Explained*. Anthony Bertram, perhaps the most prolific design writer of the period, was
working on *Design in Daily Life*. Noel Carrington wrote books on
Design in the Home and *Design and a Changing Civilization*, and Herbert Read's *Art and Industry* was in its first edition. Milner Gray
later wrote respectfully of Read: 'he became the acknowledged
leader, mentor and guide of such young designers as myself. This
was in many ways the turning point for most of us in the clear
understanding of machine art, as we called it then'. Brian Grant,
at the time, was a great deal more impatient, with a tirade in the
Architectural Review:

'So much chatter and so very little apparent progress.
"Design and Industry", "Art and Industry", "Art in Industry",
"Industrial Art", "Commercial Art", "Design for Living",
"Architectural Design" AND SO ON.'

But as well as all the chatter, there were some true advances.
The DIA considered training for designers; the FBI thought hard
about industrial art management. In 1934, as a result of the Gorell
Report, a Council for Art and Industry was founded, with government support, to educate consumers in design appreciation, to
consider design training for industry and commerce, to encourage
good design 'especially in relation to manufacturers'. The Chairman of the Council was Frank Pick. Its first remarks were sober:
'a long time will be required to complete the task which the
Council has set itself'. And yet despite this caution, and despite
the fact that Government support was materially meagre, morale
was raised substantially. Pick's Council was official. As they felt
in 1850, things were happening at last.

It is not, in fact, far-fetched to compare the atmosphere in the
year which led up to the Great Exhibition to the general optimism
in 1934, the year before the Royal Society of Arts' exhibition
'British Art in Industry'. This was to be held at Burlington House,
whence the Arts and Crafts had been banished by fine artists.
This was intended to impress upon the British as well as the foreign
public the importance of beauty in the articles they purchased,
and to prove to manufacturers that British artists could supply
'original, attractive and technically suitable designs for the production of articles by mechanical means'. What more could people
ask? The exhibition sounded exactly what designers had been
waiting for for years. If the director John de la Valette, a small
and volatile Dutchman with a beard, raised a few small doubts,
or the selection committee of high Academicians (even Scott and
Lutyens) caused some slight anxiety, this was not admitted, or at
least it was not publicized. Everyone, serenely, was hoping for
the best.

Of course, 'British Art in Industry', just like the Great Exhibition, was a major disappointment to the British design purists. It was fanciful, extravagant, nothing to do with design for mass-production; it was totally unfunctional, completely inefficient, ladylike, directed towards Mayfair gracious living. Alas for Wells Coates and his Minimum Flat: the DIA, pride wounded, called it 'a grotesque failure'. With attacks more vitriolic than Owen Jones' or Redgrave's on the fateful Crystal Palace, the critics soon let fly. Herbert Read, with the excuse that the exhibition would do more harm than good unless it was demolished, went on to lash out at a bed by Betty Joel: 'It is made of beautiful Queensland walnut and maple twisted and contorted into a shape which I can only compare to a dislocated hip-bath.' Everywhere, the lack of form and functional efficiency very much distressed him; even Heal's, he said, had become 'modish and Mayfairish'; the elegant design in icing sugar by Mr Rex Whistler reduced him to silence; he was dreadfully unnerved. In the *New Statesman*, Raymond Mortimer insisted the exhibition was worse than none at all: 'the standards it sets are both costly and depraved'. Even Nikolaus Pevsner, a recent refugee who was treading rather carefully, not hurting people's feelings, admitted that the exhibition was embarrassing for anyone with foreign visitors in London: 'Yet,' he kindly commented, 'what such an exhibition might have been! It might have set up a milestone in the evolution of the Modern Movement in England.'

And, in a way, it did. For as the Crystal Palace had caused the Cole reformers to pause, take stock and start on a new constructive phase, this latest grotesque failure, which sent shudders down the spine of the British modern movement, was in the end quite useful. It stimulated action. For instance, J. M. Richards, then assistant editor of the *Architectural Review*, taken to task for his obstructionist attitude by Burlington House showmen and friends of de la Valette, wrote a long, important, thoughtful and of course defensive article, 'Towards a Rational Aesthetic'. This examined the character of modern industrial design, showing how it differed from handicraft design, arguing that it entails a changed vocabulary in conformity with a new unity of values. It insists upon simplicity and it emphasizes the impersonal. But standardization does not mean monotony: J. M. Richards was insistent on this point. He gave some illustrations of the rational aesthetic: a strong-room door showing 'the beauty of mechanical precision', laboratory glass, porcelain vessels by Doulton and Royal Worcester, an Imperial Airways monoplane, a Rolls Royce. He added a catalogue of everyday objects generally available: Anglepoise lamps, sports equipment from Fortnum & Mason, assorted baths and basins, kitchen cabinets and cookers, stoneware footwarmers, cane carpet-beaters, metal chairs and tools, 'everyday things in which a high standard of design has been unselfconsciously achieved'. Like Semper and Matthew Digby Wyatt, he had listed the ordinary products which do not strive for art.

What was most ironic was the way in which these everyday utilitarian objects became themselves a cult. Royal Doulton's Acid Jars were sold by Gordon Russell as objects of beauty to adorn the house, and Pevsner, in *Industrial Art in England*, published in 1937, states, 'At present they are amongst the best-sellers in most shops dealing in well-designed modern goods.' The same was true of Cornish Ware, which leads one to suspect that the peasant-life fixation was not so deeply buried. It was not wholly banished by the rational aesthetic, and in the post-war years it was to recur again.

Ironically, also, the drive for anonymity was largely the concern of a few dozen individuals who were quite outstanding, even manic, in their efforts. Shipowner Colin Anderson comes straightaway to mind. Though his family, the partners in the Orient Line, were hardly inartistic (Kenneth Anderson, a relative, had been the first Chairman of the DIA), their ideas on the design of the interiors of passenger ships seemed antiquated to him, in 1930. He made up his mind 'to meet the unexpressed need of the travelling public for surroundings that looked more in keeping with the practical achievements of modern engineer-constructors'. He was so persuasive, or so tiresomely insistent, that his elders handed the whole job on to him. Considering Wells Coates, Hill and Maufe and Serge Chermayeff, all of whom seemed then to him a little disconcerting, he chose as his designer Brian O'Rorke, a good outsider, a New Zealand architect with almost nothing to his name. Architect and client, who were then both twenty-eight, agreed extremely well; they were both of them determined to escape from damask patterns, floral sprigs and sprays, cut velvet, plush and chintz, and brass and bobbles and the vaguely Louis cutlery, traditional paraphernalia of ship decor. The 'Orion', delivered in 1935, and the 'Orcades', completed in 1937, set a startlingly new standard, both of overall design and of fixtures and fittings meticulously chosen. Colin Anderson wrote later:
'It would be hard to exaggerate the difficulties we met in persuading proud and successful industries that not a single object in their entire output was acceptable for a modern ship interior. We found ourselves having to discover designers capable of producing new designs for a wide range of products, from carpets to cutlery, the makers of which had no staff designers who understood what we were after.'
He employed, among others, E. McKnight Kauffer, Marion Dorn, Alastair Morton of Edinburgh Weavers; Brian O'Rorke designed the furniture and chairs, which were heavily tested by the Orient directors. Such courage and such competence, two Empire-building qualities diverted to the modern movement, stood it in good stead. The 'Orion' and 'Orcades'—like the BBC interiors of

1932 by McGrath, Coates and Chermayeff—altered the outlook of industry a little, just perceptibly broadening its mind.

Such as it was, the British modern movement in industrial design was wholly individual enterprise, involving a handful of impresarios, like Anderson and Pick (by then with London Transport); a few designers, a few manufacturers and, increasingly important, a few enlightened shopkeepers. The tinyness of movements for improvement was made obvious in Pevsner's *Industrial Art in England*, a survey carried out at Birmingham University, under Professor Sargent Florence. A conscientious plod round 149 manufacturers, 15 shops, 14 art schools, and 17 designers, artists and architects proved that things in general were extremely bad. 'When I say,' said Pevsner, 'that 90 per cent of British industrial art is devoid of any aesthetic merit I am not exaggerating . . . the aim of any campaign for better design can only be to reduce the percentage of objectionable goods, from 90 to 80 or perhaps 75 per cent.'

It might have been a losing battle. All the same, and in spite of Pevsner's words of warning, people thought it worth a try. Wherever there was progress, this progress could be traced back to just one person fighting the great tide, or as Gordon Russell put it, pushing a tank fanatically uphill. The designers pushing tanks were the Russells, Robert Goodden, Alfred Read, Keith Murray, Enid Marx, Marian Pepler (later Mrs R. D. Russell), Marion Dorn, Marianne Straub—in her 70 Welsh textile mills—Chermayeff, Coates, McGrath. As these were mainly architects, design for industry was a spare-time occupation in nine cases out of ten.

The manufacturers were, once again, the Russells; Jack Pritchard (Isokon); Gerald Summers (The Makers of Simple Furniture of Charlotte Street); Thomas Barlow of Barlow & Jones; Allan Walton Textiles; Sir James Morton of Edinburgh Weavers; the potter Susie Cooper; on the whole, Josiah Wedgwood; and three leading makers of light fittings, the Boissevains of Merchant Adventurers, Robert Best of Best & Lloyd and H. T. Young of Troughton & Young, who from the beginning was employing A. B. Read.

The shopkeepers included (from the old days) Ambrose Heal and more recently, his sons Anthony and Christopher, who joined the firm in 1934 and two years later was showing his designs, alongside Breuer, Fry, McGrath, Nicholson, O'Rorke and Jack Howe, in an exhibition entitled 'Seven Architects'. In Bristol, Crofton Gane, that very enterprising retailer, commissioned a pavilion for the Bristol Royal Show from Yorke and Marcel Breuer, late of the Bauhaus, by then practising in Britain. Gordon Russell's shop in Wigmore Street was, to all intents and purposes, an embryo Design Centre, and famous in its day. In Hitchin, Frank Austin and, in London, Ian Henderson and Alister Maynard were selling hand-made furniture of their own design. Peter Jones had an exclusive range of modern craftsman's furniture designed and made by R. Gordon Stark. George Breeze at Lewis's and Victor Sawtell at Bowman's, Camden Town, ran furniture departments of a popular modernity and a very reasonable standard of design. It was Sawtell who promoted the first unit furniture developed in Britain by Alpe Brothers of Banbury.

In Grosvenor Street, Cecilia Dunbar (now Lady Sempill) opened an exclusive shop with Athole Hay, Royal College of Art registrar. He sent her his students, and she placed their designs for china, glass, textiles and even carpets with co-operative firms. Four-fifths of the stock at Dunbar-Hay was specially made; in those days even Wedgwood would take on special orders. Eric Ravilious, who was retained by Dunbar-Hay, decorated Wedgwood urns and mugs with great inventiveness. and also designed glass, a dining-table and some chairs which were bought by the Victoria and Albert Museum.

In Bromley, Geoffrey Dunn, with the same enthusiasm but less rarified ambitions, joined his father's firm at the age of 23 and spent £10, illicitly, on Susie Cooper pottery which he then displayed, among the reproduction furniture, on hessian-covered cubes. It was all sold in three weeks. The Bromley modern movement went from strength to strength: by 1938, the shop was almost wholly modern. In 1938, Geoffrey Dunn and Crofton Gane and Gordon Russell, with the fine old British mixture of high ideals and *bonhomie*, had formed the Good Furniture Group. This was an association of retailers which collectively commissioned designs, had them manufactured and stocked them simultaneously: the simple aim, wrote Dunn, was 'to get some nice furniture designed and made and sold by a few real believers'. The most successful project was a dining suite: good furniture from Gordon Russell Limited.

Pleasant and straightforward, civilized and sensible, a reasonably idealistic, gentlemanly clique: the Good Furniture Group was a very true reflection of the British modern movement by 1938. In fact, the modern movement had come and almost gone again; the rational aesthetic had not really made much headway. Industrial design was still quite homespun in its attitudes, not so very far from the British Arts and Crafts: tolerant and gentle, unpretentious and careful, in friendly and predictable agreement with Frank Pick that national design should be 'modest and not too grandiose in scale . . . not too logical in form . . . a reasonable compromise between beauty and utility, neither overstressing beauty till it degenerates into ornament, nor overstressing utility until it becomes bare and hard'.

This is why Great Britain could not really stand the Bauhaus. Gropius' arrival, sponsored by Jack Pritchard, escaping from the Nazis in 1934, brought the British face-to-face with what had been a far-off theory. And on the whole they realized that it was not for them. It was too unnerving; it was too uncompromising; Gropius' belief that crafts and industry were opposites and handicrafts' sole function was industrial research, that handicrafts belonged in the factory laboratory, was a good deal too dogmatic for the British DIA. And the British DIA, in its turn, unnerved Gropius with its slowness and its politeness and extreme naivety. In Birmingham a member asked to see the Bauhaus timetable, thinking that it might be applied to the teaching at the Birmingham College of Arts and Crafts. Gropius was horrified: 'It would not tell you much,' he replied with deepest scorn, 'it was the *atmosphere*.' The difference of opinion, and simple lack of work, drove Gropius out of England: in partnership with Fry, he had only been commissioned to design one house, one college, and a few small oddments, a fire for Best & Lloyd and an aluminium waste-bin. Like Breuer and Moholy-Nagy, Eric Mendelsohn, Serge Chermayeff and Naum Gabo, Walter Gropius left Britain for America. He had been appointed Harvard Professor of Architecture. People said how sad they were, and even how surprised. Herbert Read and other mourners wrote a letter to *The Times* in a rather aggrieved tone:

'Professor Gropius has been resident in this country for the last three years, and it was the confident hope of many people that we were to have the benefit of his outstanding talents for many years to come. In this we have been disappointed.'

However, they gave Gropius a Trocadero dinner (25s a head, including wine) and settled back quite equably into the old routine.

Almost as a send-off to Gropius, and a sign of relief that the old order was unchanged, the British created some Royal Designers for Industry. Excited by the 1935 Exhibition of 'British Art in Industry' at Burlington House, the Royal Society of Arts had decided to decorate designers who consistently produced work of a high aesthetic standard, and set them on a level with the Royal Academicians. In 1936, ten Designers for Industry were formally appointed, and in 1937 the Home Office decreed that these Designers should be Royal. They were an odd collection: poster artists and typographers, decorators, old-time craftsmen, Eric Gill who hated factories, Keith Murray, Harold Stabler, aged Voysey—although Voysey loathed the modern movement, which he found unchristian.

The Faculty of Royal Designers for Industry—which still goes on, enlarged and a bit more level-headed—includes a little section for Honorary Members, distinguished industrial designers from abroad. Through the years, these foreign appointments have shown neatly the current allegiances of design in Britain. In 1939, for instance, before Alvar Aalto or Gropius was honoured, Raymond Loewy (USA) was received into the Faculty. This was an event of some significance. For it meant the recognition of the 'stylists' of America, the large expansive prophets of commercial design, Bel Geddes and van Doren, Dorwin Teague and Henry Dreyfuss who, like Loewy, had been spending the past decade in league with the great advertising agencies, promoting the idea that design is businesslike. An RDI for Loewy meant acceptance of the fact that design in Britain, too, was increasingly commercial: in Loewy's British office (with J. Beresford-Evans, Douglas Scott and F. C. Ashford), in Richard Lonsdale-Hands' thrusting new Design Unit, and the group which Norbert Dutton, Ronald Armstrong and Ronald Ingles had founded very recently, all leaving Metal Box. This regime meant rejection, or at least ruthless dilution of the DIA virtues and the old crusading zeal. As Milner Gray, in a later speech, expressed it:

'From the cosy gatherings of the converted and the high ideals of the highbrows of the 1920s, industrial design had come down to earth.'

But it did not stay there long. With the war, a time of fantasy, the businesslike designers, architects and art directors were hurried into uniform and set to work to hide the defences of the country as soon as they were built. The *Architectural Review* gave fine descriptions of the work of Her Majesty's Camouflage Corps in disguising the ubiquitous hexagonal pillboxes as tea-kiosks, bus stops, petrol stations, fair booths and public lavatories, as haystacks, road-menders' huts and even wood-piles. Wartime, for designers, was a kind of golden age in which almost unlimited money and labour were forthcoming to pursue the wildest fancies, masterpieces of inventiveness, from ivy-clad ruins to gypsy caravans, from cosy thatched toll-houses to resplendent Gothic lodge-gates. All this was perfect practice for the Festival of Britain, and helps greatly to explain the light fantastic atmosphere.

99

100

99
Marcel Breuer
Long chair in laminated birch made by Isokon, 1936.

100
Gerald Summers
Chair in laminated birch made by the Makers of Simple Furniture, Charlotte Street, about 1934.

101
Gordon Russell
'Weston' dining furniture in oak, 1929.

102
R. D. Russell
'Thirty-Four' unit bedroom furniture in oak, made by Gordon Russell Furniture, 1934.

101

102

103

104

105

106

103
Alpe Brothers
Dining group including waxed oak
furniture sold at Dunn's of Bromley,
1935.

104
Geoffrey Dunn
Bookcase and desk, with other
furniture sold at Dunn's of Bromley,
1934.

105
Wells Coates
Radio cabinet in bakelite made by
Ecko, 1934.

106
R. D. Russell
Radio cabinet made by Murphy in
light walnut with dark stained sides,
1937.

107
R. D. Russell
Sideboard in Bombay rosewood with
elm lines made by Gordon Russell
Furniture, 1935.

107

108
Serge Chermayeff
Stacking chair for Broadcasting House, 1932.

109
Serge Chermayeff
Interior of flat at 42 Upper Brook Street, W.1., 1935.

110
Serge Chermayeff
Stacking chair for Broadcasting House, 1932.

111
Raymond McGrath
Balcony doors to Studio BB, Broadcasting House, 1932.

112
Raymond McGrath
Studio BB, Broadcasting House, 1932.

110

111   112

113

114

113
Maxwell Fry and Jack Howe
Living room from Heal's
'7 Architects Exhibition', 1936.

114
Walter Gropius
Waste-paper basket in perforated
aluminium sold by Gordon Russell
Ltd., 1937.

115
Brian O'Rorke
First-class lounge on Orient liner
Orion, 1935.

116
Brian O'Rorke
First-class café on Orient liner
Orion, 1935.

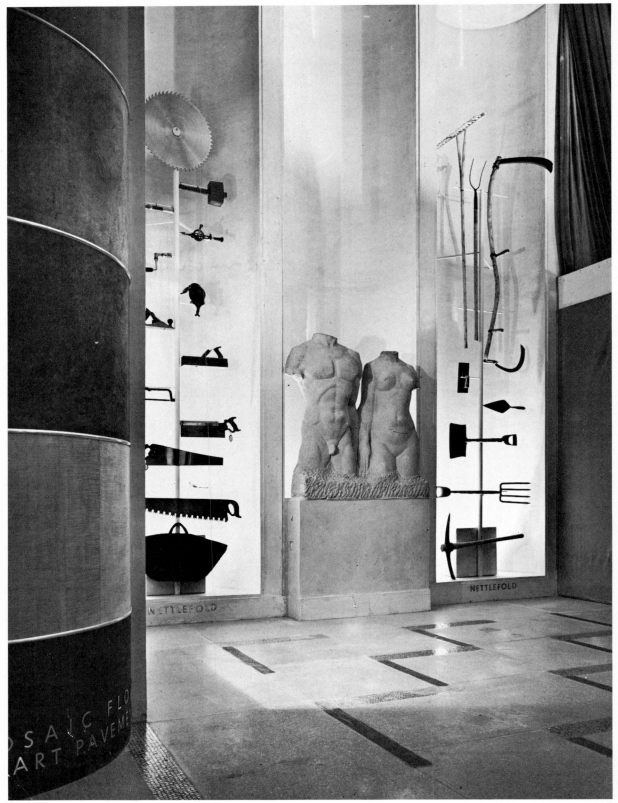

NETTLEFOLD

NETTLEFOLD

MOSAIC FLO
ART PAVEME

STONE
ENGRAVED DRAWINGS BY ERIC GILL · STONE BY JENKINS AND SON

JADE
ED BY THE
N GALLERY

119

120

117
Design and Industries Association
Entrance vestibule, Dorland Hall
Exhibition, 1933.

118
Design and Industries Association
Dining room furniture in Portland
stone, Dorland Hall Exhibition,
1933.

119
London Transport
Bus shelter, 1939.

120
London Transport
Leicester Square Underground
Booking Hall, 1935.

121
London Transport
Staircase on LT-type bus, 1931.

122

123

124

125

126

122
London Transport
Trolleybus, 1939.

123
London Transport
Tube train interior, 1938.

124, 125 and 126
Marion Dorn
Upholstery fabrics for London
Transport, 1939.

127

128

129

130

131

127
Marian Pepler
'Wood Ash' tufted rug, about 1933.

128
Marian Pepler
'45' tufted rug, about 1933.

129
Paul Nash
'Fugue' screen-printed linen, 1936.

130
Marianne Straub
Furnishing fabric, cotton and fibro,
made by Helios, 1939.

131
Duncan Grant
Hand-printed artificial silk made by
Allan Walton, 1932.

132
Duncan Grant
Screen-printed cotton satin made by
Allan Walton, 1938.

132

133

133
Keith Murray
Decanter and glasses made by
Stevens & Williams, about 1935.

134
Keith Murray
Earthenware beer mugs and jug
made by Wedgwood, 1935.

135
Keith Murray
Cocktail set and silver bowl made by
Mappin and Webb, 1935.

136
Keith Murray
Cocktail cups, matt white
earthenware with platinum bands,
made by Wedgwood, 1935.

137

138

137
Eric Ravilious
'Boat Race' bowl in earthenware with transfer prints, made by Wedgwood, 1938.

138
Susie Cooper
'Beechwood' hand-painted plate and tea cup, 1937.

139
Joseph Bourne
Fireproof earthenware casseroles, about 1935.

139

140

140
Eric Ravilious
'Garden Implements' mugs and jug
made by Wedgwood, late 1930s.

141
Milner Gray (three top designs) *and*
Graham Sutherland
Decoration for bone china for Foley
China, E. Brain & Co., 1935.

142

143

144

142
R. Y. Goodden
Small pressed glass bowl made by
Chance Brothers, 1934.

143
R. Y. Goodden
Pressed glass powder bowl made by
Chance Brothers, 1935.

144
Graham Sutherland
Decorated glassware made by
Stuart Crystal, 1935.

145
Milner Gray
Silver porringer and spoon for
D. & J. Wellby, 1946.

146
Milner Gray
Bottle and label for a ginger barley
wine for Clark's Creamed Barley,
1937.

147
Milner Gray
Stoneware wine jar and label made
for Mid-Sussex Canning and
Preserving Co., 1935.

145

146   147

148

149

150

148
Best and Lloyd
'Bestlite' reading lamp, 1930.

149
A. B. Read
'Ultralux' light fitting made by
Troughton and Young, about 1930.

150
A. B. Read
'Ultralux' light fitting made by
Troughton and Young, about 1930.

151
E. S. Corner
Escor 7-seater car, late 1930s.

152
John Waterer
'Vogue' lightweight luggage in
cowhide made by S. Clarke, about
1937.

5
The Council of Industrial Design 1940-1951

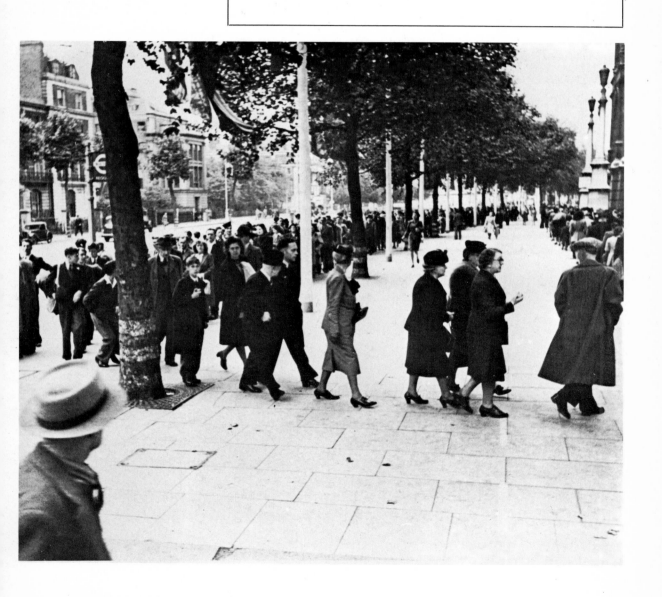

IT was 1942 when Gordon Russell's country war-work, stone-carving, looking after bees and keeping pigs, was for ever interrupted: Hugh Dalton wrote requesting him to sit on a Utility furniture committee. Although he did not realize it, this sudden translation from the Cotswolds to an office at the Board of Trade would have long repercussions, both for him and for the progress of industrial design. Under Gordon Russell a new reform began, related to the earlier attempts, yet very different in its scope, organization and its government support. Government furniture was more or less a godsend. 'I felt,' wrote Gordon Russell, 'that to raise the whole standard of furniture for the mass of the people was not a bad war-job . . . Wartime conditions had given us a unique opportunity of making an advance.'

There had been an ultimatum: from November 1942 the only furniture to be manufactured in Britain was Utility. Hundreds of small firms throughout the country, with all kinds of methods of production, would then make a single range of furniture under the control of a central small committee. Dalton had selected this committee with finesse. Counteracting Russell there was Lebus, mass-producer; balancing John Gloag and Elizabeth Denby there was Mrs Wimborne and the Reverend Jenkinson, the voice of the consumer and presumably the church; there was trade and there was public, there were housing men and retailers, a beautiful cross-section of the national state of taste. Gordon Russell travelled up to London for the first of the meetings; with the deadline in November, it was by then July.

The President of the Board of Trade, Hugh Dalton, came in to his committee with some rules and regulations: Utility furniture must be soundly made of the best possible materials; it must be pleasant in design; and it must also be produced extremely quickly, to prevent a national famine. He departed very briskly, leaving the committee with a long list of materials, everything they needed, from plywood and blockboard to steel and paint and textiles, which were either unobtainable or else extremely scarce. He also left them puzzling over what he meant by pleasant: in common usage, 'pleasant' furniture was Jacobean. But—first round to Gordon Russell—as he wrote, 'the basic rightness of contemporary design won the day'. There was not enough timber for bulbous legs or labour for even the most rudimentary carving. Mr Clinch and Mr Cutler, stout designers from High Wycombe, evolved for new Utility a modern Gimson style, which the *Architectural Review* attacked as retrograde (too true to the DIA, too fit and far too honest), and the trade on the whole condemned as too advanced. Gordon Russell was contented to see shots from both directions: 'it looked', he recollected 'as if we were about right. I am never for forcing the pace, a limited advance and then consolidation is a sound principle, both in war and peace'. This calm, most British, attitude was usefully disarming in peacetime at the

Council of Industrial Design.

Meanwhile, Gordon Russell wrote a report—as Cole would have done—to his chairman, Charles Tennyson, whose work for the FBI Committee on design and the wartime Central Institute had proved him sympathetic. Gordon Russell suggested a programme of research into furniture design, for wartime use and for the future; he recommended a panel of not more than six designers with a knowledgeable chairman, probably an architect, who would be given a seat on the Utility Furniture Committee to speak for the designers. To Gordon Russell's suprise, the President asked him to take on the Chairman's job himself and set about appointing the members of the Panel. This, in fact, was none too easy for the best of the designers were abroad or inaccessible. Eden Minns, who had agreed to join, was without warning called up into the Navy and sent out to the Pacific; Dick Russell was in Admiralty camouflage and rapidly transported off to India and Burma; Ian Henderson, who thought the Foreign Office might have loaned him, found the scheme impracticable. But Jacques Groag, a Czech refugee, an architect and former pupil and assistant of Adolf Loos, was a most imaginative, vociferous addition to the Panel, counteracting the prosaic, though most worthy, Clinch and Cutler. Utility Furniture was ready to progress.

Installed at the Board of Trade, without a desk and carpet (for no one knew their status), working in a room furnished mainly with their own discarded prototypes, regarded with tender solicitude by permanent officials, even pointed out by the most venerable members as proof of what the country will resort to in a war, Gordon Russell and his Furniture Design Panel embarked on a programme of design research in two directions: into temporary furniture to cope with devastation if the bombing should intensify; and into long-term planning for furniture for peace-time, when supplies of plywood, blockboard, cellulose and steel would be once again at hand. With a doggedness that should have made a scene for Evelyn Waugh, the Design Panel investigated consumer needs, talking to the Board of Trade, talking to the Housing Centre, finding out how people live and how they use their furniture. Gordon Russell went to Toynbee Hall to meet the Peckham residents. One of them kept nothing but her knitting in a sideboard. Another complained fiercely that a piece of bombed-out glass had gone through the end of her Utility Furniture: 'You can't call that a piece of furniture,' she said. A black-eyed, hawk-nosed woman got up and asked the Panel whether Utility furniture would stand up to it. Stand up to what? She beat around the bush, then admitted that the furniture in question was the bed.

There were worries. Plain Utility shapes were sometimes decorated, under the counter, with the most appalling carving. The Committee, trying to meet the public need for a bit of wartime gaiety, discussed the possibility of a patterned range, taking up their problem with the sculptor Henry Moore whose interest in abstract patterns was well known. But Moore, though very willing, had nothing to contribute. Utility furniture remained plain solid modern, with a clodhopping character, until the war was ending, and the mass-production woodworking firms employed on aircraft could return to furniture. The Panel then developed a range of smaller, lighter, more sophisticated and more graceful furniture. To a chorus of approval from even the *Architectural Review*, the latest Utility range was unveiled on VE Day at a CEMA exhibition in the National Gallery: 'Some pieces such as a mahogany sideboard and some easy chairs are very attractive indeed.'

Gordon Russell's war-work had substantial influence, after an initial frenzied contrary reaction to Utility design, on the general run of furniture: within another fifteen years, plain Gimson-style was fashion. Gordon Russell set the scene for the general reformation of design in post-war Britain soberly, humanely, subtly, with a good use of committees, with a constant view to 'solid, not spectacular, progress'. From now on, and for many years, this was the general aim of the leaders of the movement. Designers emerged, like Gordon Russell, from their war-work with a new determination and realistic aims. Besides the Camouflagers, who were legion, there were others: Jack Howe, for example, had been drawing office manager for Royal Ordnance factories; Douglas Scott and Richard Huws had worked with aircraft firms; Jack Proctor had been trained in basic engineering, at the government's expense; Robert Cantor had learned about industrial design from working on radar instruments; and Ronald Dickens, at the request of the Fire Service Chief, and using the Hendon District Surveyor's office, had designed a blast-proof control shelter and received the personal thanks of Herbert Morrison. Kenneth Holmes, the Art School Principal at Leicester, was responsible for refurnishing the City General Hospital, organizing city-wide voluntary labour for the making of splints and urgent hospital equipment; plaster bandaging for Leicester and its environs was made, and sent out by the boxful, from the College of Art.

None of this was wartime wasted. In the Ministry of Information, Exhibitions Division, Milner Gray and Misha Black and Kenneth Bayes together made good use of their time. In the intervals of planning patriotic exhibitions, they evolved a new design group the size and scope of which had not been known in Britain, or this side of the Atlantic. As early as 1942, the aims and organization of Design Research Unit had been formulated by Milner Gray: in general,

'The purpose of the formation of a group such as is envisaged is to make available immediately a design service equipped to advise on all problems of design and to form a nucleus group which through contacts established during the war period with specialist designers and experts in all appropriate fields, would be in a position at the end of the war to expand to undertake the wider services which may then be demanded of it.

'The final aim is to present a service so complete that it could undertake any design case which might confront the State, Municipal Authorities, Industry or Commerce.

'The scope of such a service would be so wide, within its sphere, that any description may seem to imply a limitation. But it is perhaps useful to remind ourselves of some of the fields of operation open to such an organization. All productions of industry necessary to the home life of the community and to the public services come properly within the purview of such a group. Every garment which we wear, every utensil that we use, every notice that we read, every service in transport and in our daily round of which we make use. Design for the banks, breweries, petrol, shipping and co-operative companies: design for Government printing, publicity and exhibitions: design for office, shop and warehouse: design for the lamp standard, the fire alarm, the letter-box, street name plates, traffic signs and traffic control box: design for the packing of products: design for kitchen, household and hotel equipment. Everything that is made is first designed.'

Although it seems impossible, an even vaster scheme for design was then afoot within the Board of Trade, involving Laurence Watkinson and Alan Hoskin, involving Francis Meynell (temporary adviser on Civilian Needs), involving Thomas Barlow (Director- General of Civilian Clothing) and, from time to time, involving Gordon Russell, at work among his prototypes along the corridor. The idea was a Council. Not a Council like Frank Pick's understaffed and undersubsidized and rather unconvincing, but a Central Design Council big enough and strong enough to raise the design standards in industry at large, with the ultimate purpose of improving British exports. The details were decided long before the war had ended. In 1943 Cecil Weir's Sub-Committee on Industrial Design and Art in Industry (set up by the Post-War Export Trade Committee of the Department of Overseas Trade) reported that since there *is* such a thing as recognizably good design, and since there *is not* a fundamental conflict between 'giving the public what it wants' and good design, then a Central Design Council, not directly responsible to a government department, should start work. In 1944, the Meynell-Hoskin Report (submitted to the Presidents of the Boards of Trade and Education) discussed ways and means of making art training more practical and useful for the 'post-war push', and recommended that the Central Design Council should be a grant-aided body, financed on the Board of Trade vote. This should all be discussed with the Ministry of Reconstruction, they said: and it was. And just as the FBI Industrial Art Committee was completing its own 'Proposals for a Central

Design Council and Industrial Design Centre', the Coalition
Government had moved ahead.

'Has the President of the Board of Trade,' asked John Dugdale in
Parliament on 19 December 1944, 'taken steps to encourage good
design in British industry?'

'Yes sir,' said Dr Hugh Dalton. 'I have appointed a Council of
Industrial Design to promote by all practicable means the
improvement of design in the products of British industry.'

With that assurance, the Government went on to consider
British Engines (Spare Parts) and Discharged Service Men
(Badge): the Prime Minister maintaining that no man's patriotism
could be challenged because he wore civilian clothes.

One has to remember the emotions of the period, the surging
hopefulness, the urge for great renewal, the feeling that the man
and the woman in the street deserved a better life, deserved improved design. All this comes pounding through the speech which
Dr Hugh Dalton made to his new Council in 1944:

'We must, therefore, make a sustained effort to improve design,
and to bring industry to recognize the importance of this task.
You have to arouse the interest of ordinary men and women . . .
If you succeed in your task, in a few years' time every side of our
daily life will be better for your work. Every kitchen will be an
easier place to work in; every home a pleasanter place to live in.
Men and women in millions will be in your debt, though they
may not know it; and not in Britain alone but all over the world.
. . . Industry itself will have much cause to thank you. Our export
trade, and our volume of business at home, will both be the greater
if our goods are planned and made, with skill and imagination,
to meet the user's real need, to give pleasure in the using.'

Listening, and taking note were the two dozen first members of
the Council, including Francis Meynell, Ernest Goodale, Charles
Tennyson, Josiah Wedgwood, Allan Walton, Gordon Russell (all
old aesthetic warriors). The Chairman was Sir Thomas Barlow.
The Director was S. C. Leslie, who came to the CoID from the
Home Office, where he was Principal Assistant Secretary. Though
hardly a DIA tub-thumper in his outlook, he was not inartistic.
He soon learned about design.

The Government had changed, as governments will change—
often spelling doom to small grant-aided bodies. But the Council of
Industrial Design, which was the offshoot of a coalition government, was blessedly immune, and in 1945, the election of Labour
brought an extra supporter for reformers of design. It brought
Sir Stafford Cripps, an eager weekend-carpenter, to replace Dr
Hugh Dalton at the Board of Trade. This was good for the Council
of Industrial Design, for Cripps (and Cripps' wife) had still more
heart in it than Dalton. Within twenty-four hours of his appointment, he was over at the CoID offices in Petty France telling the
Director to stage an exhibition: never mind about the money,

there would be a special grant.

With an extra £234,757; with much talk of turning swords into ploughshares and producing 'goods as suitable for peace time as were the weapons the country produced for the war', 'Britain Can Make It', a great exhibition—great for post-wartime—was rapidly planned. There had already been two excellent post-war design displays: the CEMA Exhibition 'Design in the Home' (by Milner Gray) and the substantial Exhibition of Wallpapers (displayed on Eric Brown and Stefan Buzas). But this new exhibition was to be much more ambitious. 'Britain Can Make It' was planned for 90,000 square feet of the Victoria and Albert Museum, which at the time was empty (it was also without windows: a minor difficulty which Cripps soon overcame by diverting London's next two months' entire supply of glass). It was meant 'to intensify the interest of manufacturers and distributors in industrial design, and their awareness of the desirability of rapid progress; to arouse greater interest in design in the minds of the general public, as consumers; and to stage a prestige advertisement, before the world, for British industry, industrial design and standards of display'. Cripps saw it as the first blossoming of British industry after the devastating effects of war.

This was all very well. But what was there to show? The *Architectural Review* was very nervous, suggesting that Cripps was rather overdoing things, pointing out:
'It is he who conceived the idea of the exhibition and insists on its early date. Council and manufacturers will have a tough job, with no materials yet to make new things, and no skilled labour, with plenty of designers still in the forces, with an understandable dislike to show the old 1938 things again, and an equally understandable dislike to show new designs not yet in production. What will be exhibited then? Prototypes, models, products available for export only? One feels unable even to guess, and yet one ardently wishes this test show the greatest possible international success.'

And a great success it was. Although most of the exhibits were in fact still unobtainable, although the exhibition was renamed by the public 'Britain Can't Have It', Cripps' wildest schemes were justified. It pleased a lot of people in many different ways. It was ideal for the *Architectural Review*, showing British products deprived of frills and furbelows by wartime stress and shortages, as close as they had ever been to rational aesthetics. (This was rationality perforce: it did not last.) 'Britain Can Make It' pleased the King and Queen, who made a special journey from Balmoral for the opening. It very much pleased *Punch*, which joked about the imitation farmer's bedroom designed by David Medd with a Kenneth Rowntree picture of a tractor on the wall. Most of all, and in great numbers, the Exhibition pleased the people: a million and a half formed patient queues (which they were used to) down the road as far as the Brompton Oratory, and wandered round the Exhibition with amazement, a third of a mile of it, almost in a dream.

They wandered through the Foyer designed by Basil Spence (assistant to James Gardner, Exhibition Designer). They moved into a section called 'From War to Peace' which showed 'side by side with their warlike origins' some 20 domestic articles evolved from the new processes, new materials and new techniques developed during the war: a new type of saucepan was shown beside the exhaust stub of a wrecked Spitfire, inflatable reclining chairs lined up with dummy weapons, and in case the swords-to-ploughshares theme escaped the public, the products were exhibited against a dim background of bomb-shattered London, picked out by shafts of light. On and on to the Textiles, Metal, Rubber, Glass and Timber, Plastics and Paper; to the Shop Window Street, with its hosiery display and its fanciful Glove Tree:

'On entering this section the visitor obtains his plastic coins at the QUIZ BANK on the left of a large entrance platform, paved with rubber, from which he surveys the brightly-lit displays set under a dark blue sky, charged with a faint afterglow of sunset . . . Each visitor is presented with 10 coins for QUIZ BOXES placed in various parts of the hall. Each box contains 3 photographs of comparable articles, and 3 coin slots. The visitor can thus register a "vote" for the design he favours.'

On, via Quiz Boxes, to 'Things in Their Home Setting' (commentary John Betjeman): The Working Class Utility Kitchen, the Middle Class Kitchen with Dining Recess, the Suburban Living Room for a hard-up curate (a keen naturalist and great reader) and his wife (who collects modern pottery) and his three children (who do homework in this room). On to the Dress Fabrics, displayed from winged horses in flight and from the arms of 'tree-women'. On to the Tea Lounge, a gypsy encampment in which 'the service counter takes the form of a caravan'. On to Women's Dress, beneath a vast white nylon canopy, and then to 'Things for Children', a child's bedroom 'out of the window of which a girl looks on to a garden animated by fairies, elves, frogs and suchlike creatures of a child's imagination, all attired in the newest children's wear'. Not for nothing was James Gardner Chief Development Officer for Army Camouflage during the war: in 'Britain Can Make It' he camouflaged austerity. He made a post-war fantasy. The public was convinced.

The public was also, very gently, introduced to the idea of industrial design. Designers' work was credited throughout the exhibition; at the end, beyond the Rest Lounge (designed by Robert Goodden), Misha Black told the public 'What Industrial Design Means', using simple examples to explain the way an industrial designer works and the way in which different materials and processes influence design: 'This theme is vividly illustrated in a section called "The Birth of an Eggcup". "Who designs the eggcup? Not the machine, which cannot think. The hen is partly responsible; she lays the egg to which all bowls to all eggcups must conform."' But the hero of the piece was the industrial designer. This was something which the public had, bit by bit, to learn.

'Design At Work', a follow-up, a smaller exhibition of products by Royal Designers for Industry, was held in 1948. It was jointly sponsored by the Royal Society of Arts and CoID. It had two quite important results, one very positive: Prince Philip came to it, encouraged by the painter who was working on his portrait, and from then on was a vigorous promoter of design. The other was more negative: the exhibition showed that designers for industry had very far to go. The exhibition was not bad, but it was thin. A handful of designers had done a few nice jobs. But the national limitations, cleverly glossed over at 'Britain Can Make It', were all too obvious now.

The position was this: there were not enough designers trained specifically for industrial design. The nucleus of staff designers in the country—in the Potteries for instance, in the carpet industry, in textiles and in silver—were obviously unlikely to raise standards on their own, both by reason of their skimpy, narrow-minded education and by reason of their fairly menial status in the trade. But how should they be supplemented? The National Register of Industrial Art Designers (founded in 1936 and resurrected as the Record of Designers by the CoID) showed on investigation that professional standards of practice left much to be desired. The Society of Industrial Artists' publication *Designers in Britain*, with examples of their work, proved all too plainly that in 1947 competent designers were in fact in short supply; though the spirit of the enterprise was businesslike and workmanlike, the same old names came round with disconcerting frequency. Though the influx of designers from abroad before the war and through it (Jacques Groag, for instance, George Fejer, Stefan Buzas, Margaret Leischner, Tibor Reich, Marianne Straub, Natasha Kroll, Hans Schleger, Willi de Majo, Lewis Woudhuysen and F. H. K. Henrion) enlivened the profession, there were virtually no national sources of supply for designers in the future. Although it was agreed the days for amateurs were over—an opinion reinforced by John Gloag's *Missing Technician*, published in 1944—and although by then it seemed obvious to the experts an architect's training was not ideal for design, it was difficult to know what to do about designers. Where could they be found, and how should they be taught?

For many, many years, back to Cole and even earlier, the British had been conscious of the lack of proper training for artists for industry (as they liked to call them). The Schools of Design, set up with best intentions, provided quite impractical art training, for a century. All through the 1930s the complaints accumulated: from the FBI, the DIA, Gorell and Pick, the Nugent Committee on Industrial Art Education, the Hambledon Committee on Industrial Art Education in London. They all said much the same. The system was no good: it did not produce designers of any use to industry, immediate or potential. The system must be changed. There were new laments in wartime; complaints from Meynell-Hoskin and the interdepartmental Committee on art training; a positive cry of despair from Herbert Read in the *Architectural Review*: 'The present educational system being not aesthetic, only a minority who have managed by luck or illness to escape its deadening influences show any natural desire to become artists or designers.' This was very true.

The most violent abuse, through the years, had been hurled at the Royal College of Art. It was useless: a waste of public money and a national disgrace. So said the innumerable committees of enquiry set up to consider its maladministration from the 1830s onwards; so, more or less, said Hambledon in 1936; so said Meynell-Hoskin; and so said Herbert Read. They all urged the College to return to its original function: the training of *industrial* designers. In 1946, the report *The Visual Arts*, sponsored by the Dartington Hall Trustees, still spoke extremely gloomily of amateurishness, unsuitable premises, inadequate equipment, hindering development at every turn:

'Throughout its chequered history it has never been adequately supported by the Ministry of Education . . . the College has yet to fulfil adequately its original purpose of training designers for industry.'

All these inadequacies at the RCA were more obvious because of the developments at other art schools: courses in design for machine production had begun, before the war, at Leicester and the Central, and immediately afterwards in Glasgow, although these courses at that date were still in embryo.

The state of education naturally worried the Council of Industrial Design. For how could it promote design in British industry when British designers were so few and far between? A Training Committee was appointed very quickly, and by 1946 their verdict was prepared. Robin Darwin, the Council's Education Officer, acted as Secretary and wrote the report. This report, though never published, was a most impressive document; with logic and proper common sense, it deprecated the traditional division in British education between the arts and sciences, the art schools and the technical schools, and schools of commerce and the universities. It argued the need for much broader and more realistic training for designers than there ever was before. The functions of the Royal College of Art were deeply considered, and Robin Darwin commented that 'Much would, of course, depend upon the Principal, and the initial appointment would be a factor of pivotal importance for the ultimate development of the school.'

And who was the new Principal? Who but Robin Darwin, author of the Council's large, profound report. The appointment, he said later, took him rather by surprise: he was by then Professor of Fine Art at Durham University. Gordon Russell, up in Newcastle for one of the CoID 'Design Weeks', came to dinner and they talked about the Principal's appointment, which was to be made the next Tuesday. Very casually, Darwin took a piece of paper and wrote down five conditions on which the new Principal ought to insist: these included a complete change of staff, five-year appointments (renewable) as well as the entire reorganization of the academic courses. Casually, Russell must have put the piece of paper in his pocket and gone off. For on Tuesday, the appointment day, arriving at his club in London for lunch, Robin Darwin found a summons to a meeting with John Maud; and when he reached the meeting and discovered 17 or 18 people sitting round a table, all thoroughly conversant with his views and five conditions for appointment, it was then obvious that the game was up.

On January 1, 1948, as Darwin recollected in *The Dodo and the Phoenix*, a day of dreadful wetness and coldness, the new Principal arrived at his new College, not exactly afraid of being eaten (like Lethaby) but slightly apprehensive. It was all extremely grim. The entrance hall, by any account a depressing place, was painted the deadliest and most institutional grey that the Ministry of Works could devise. There was nobody about, except two aged stewards playing shove ha'penny on the second floor. On his desk he found an oblong green official attendance book: the elder of the aged stewards said that in it Darwin must record the times of his arrivals and departures. The Principal quite crossly threw it in the bin, from which it was retrieved by the same steward who, instructed by the Ministry of Education, himself took note of Darwin's entrances and exits until finally the Principal, in utter desperation, was forced to tear the awful green oblong book in half.

Conditions in the College were amazing. The buildings had in 1911 been thoroughly condemned as 'unworthy of a national establishment'; in 1948 the College was still kept in a series of shacks scattered round South Kensington, without a lecture theatre, and almost without studios. A ramshackle tin drill hall, a Boer War relic, still served as the students' all-purpose common room. The drawing desks were stamped 1870; the looms for students of weaving were even more historic; the printed textiles students were reduced to using Morrison shelters for tables; and worse, there was only one sewing-machine to be shared between all unfortunate students of Dress. Conditions were so frightful that William Rothenstein, Principal in 1920, had decided, rather

than embark on an ever-losing battle, to concentrate on painting
and forget about design.

The staff was just as primitive. Jowett, Darwin's predecessor,
asked him to tea to meet them in a body. According to Darwin,
some had never met before and many of them did not know their
colleagues' names at all. The Council of the College had no set
terms of reference, and seemed to be discouragingly blank about
finances. The pupils, up to then, had all been pre-selected not by
the professors, but by the outside visitor. All this must be changed.
As luck would have it, Robin Darwin was related to John Maud—
later Lord Redcliffe-Maud, and at that time in a powerful position at the Ministry of Education—and began negotiations for
reforms with great determination and a fair degree of confidence.

Maxwell Hyslop, a Ministry official, who just then was con-
valescing from a rather serious illness, had been given what were
classed as light Ministerial duties: responsibility for three so-
called gentle subjects: Women, Agriculture and the RCA. He
cannot have found Darwin an aid to convalescence, for the regime
now demanded for the College was quite new. Darwin wanted
(and received) full academic freedom, with the right for the
College to choose its own students, devise its own teaching methods,
frame its own examinations, grant its own awards; in addition,
the right for teaching members to select their own colleagues
without outside interference; in addition, the sharing of financial
responsibility (consistent with the use of public funds) between
the Council and Principal and staff. The Principal himself should
decide broad lines of policy in conjunction with the Council and
should provide general and if possible equal inspiration to departments in his care. Beyond this his job was mainly 'to support
his staff and act as a guardian and a watchdog of their freedom'.

One of Darwin's innovations was this dependence on, and great
faith in, his staff: he said, 'Herein must lie the real power and
vitality—and if the power is not real, the vitality will not spark.'
A bit like Cole in theory, but more pertinent in practice, he
appointed as Professors active practising designers. He equipped
the design schools for actual production: again like Henry Cole,
who had had a scheme for students making government furnishings, and like Cole's friend William Dyce who, attempting to be
practical, had brought in a loom and a Jacquard machine.
But where Cole's and Dyce's training schemes, so admirable in
principle, collapsed or were diluted, Darwin pushed his through.
And in point of fact the Cole group was never in the minds of
reformers of the College in 1948. In those days it was the Bauhaus,
with its emphasis on knowledge of materials in training for industrial design, and its well-established principle of working on
professional commissions in the classroom, which so excited
them.

In a way, the Bauhaus principles seemed to them ideal. But

these of course were tempered, as they always have been tempered, by a very British, civilized and gentlemanly attitude. It was Darwin's idea to send out from his college people with broad interests and deep sophistication, people whose minds were 'amused and well-tempered', literate, articulate and generally cultured. This traditional university ideal of a total education was well-expressed by Darwin, in superb romantic flight, in an address to the Royal Society of Arts. He explained that he had spent much of his childhood up in Cambridge. He continued:

'As I came back on a winter's evening from children's parties through the great court of Trinity or through King's, the windows of the Chapel would still be glowing from the candles lit for Evensong, with lights twinkling in the fellows' rooms upon all sides. The power that has kept them shining day in, day out, for six centuries and more, depends on the deep impulse which makes mature men come together in one place and associate with one another in learning and research, and in the common pursuit of ideas more important than themselves . . . This is the spirit which hallows all universities and gives them their timeless traditions, and I believe something of this spirit has begun to move within the Royal College of Art.'

And probably it had. Gordon Russell, with a comparable taste for the timeless traditions of the land, was certainly delighted by Darwin's appointment, and especially pleased that the announcement appeared in *The Times* on the day that Russell's own appointment as Director of the CoID became official, Clem Leslie having moved to a more straightforward job as Director of Information at the Treasury. The announcements in *The Times* were printed side-by-side, with a great sense of occasion: for this was the beginning of strong and, on the whole, affectionate ties between the CoID and the College. To start with, Gordon Russell's brother Dick was now Professor of Wood, Metal and Plastics (a temporary School which was later divided into Furniture Design, still under R. D. Russell, and design for Engineering). Robert Goodden, a great friend and ally of the Russells, was Professor of Silversmithing, Jewellery and Glass, and later the Vice-Principal. Gordon Russell recollected how, in times of trouble at the Council of Industrial Design, he could easily be comforted by the arrival of the regular pink list, beautifully illustrated and composed by Edward Ardizzone, of wines just purchased for the College Senior Common Room. Despite the fact that Gatti's, haunt of Morris and his confreres, had now been designated a club for H.M. forces, a little of the Arts and Crafts delight in proper living, good food and wine and fellowship, lingered nicely on.

Gordon Russell needed comforts: at the time when he took over at the CoID, the situation was not promising. As he said, he got the backwash from Utility furniture and from 'Britain Can Make It'. The trade—all the trades put together—disliked the idea of outside selection, as of course they always had: their order books were full, in the spate of post-war buying, and they argued very crossly that what sold was well-designed. The retailers were angry at aspersions being cast on their own ability to choose the finest products. Designers were annoyed because they felt the Council's standards were too lenient; the trade thought them ridiculously high. There was trouble from the people who were not Council-members, and insisted that they ought to be; and there was yet more trouble from people on the Council who felt that it should work at simple sales promotion, never mind about design. The trade press fought the Council, and Russell was alarmed in case the export trades united to denounce the Council's work to the Board of Trade, maintaining that the Council was jeopardizing exports by criticizing products which were bringing income in. On top of this the Chairman, Thomas Barlow, wrote resigning because of overwork.

'My army experience stood me in good stead,' wrote Gordon Russell, reminiscing on this period when rebellion was rife and there were traitors in the camp and the battle for improvement of design was fierce and endless. He left his forces fighting, and went off to Kew Gardens and drafted a plan for Council development, a good efficient plan by means of which the Council managed in the end to effect a kind of truce. In the Annual Report 1948–1949, he explained how and why he had now regrouped his staff (which for Britain Can Make It had worked in one big body) into two divisions:

'Without an effective demand for better design there can be no adequate supply of it and without examples of good design being put before the public there can be no standard of comparison on which to base the demand. The twin drive for better design must therefore be pursued at the same time—the Industrial Division, to encourage a supply of well-designed products from, and the flow of trained talent to, industry, and the Information Division to stimulate public demand for higher standards.'

Chief Industrial Officer was Mark Hartland Thomas; Chief Information Officer was Paul Reilly, son of Sir Charles Reilly, the pre-war Professor of Architecture at Liverpool University.

Convincing by showing, reforming by exhibiting, encouraging industry to mend its ways; this was nothing new. It was just what Henry Cole, Gottfried Semper and Prince Albert had been setting out to do; and the DIA, and Pick's sadly ineffective Council. And nothing much had altered; very little had improved. Gordon Russell, undeterred, with the added great advantage of a grant of £164,000 and a staff of 165, started off again to end the ever-lasting circle of apathetic manufacturers and shopkeepers and ignorant consumers. He was systematic. While industrial officers went round the manufacturers, examining, entreating and jollying along, the Information Division was travelling the country, enlightening the people, in a kind of caravan: taking its Design Fair, a mobile exhibition, to join in such civic displays as 'Sheffield on Its Mettle'; creating whole Design Weeks in Newcastle and Nottingham, Southampton, Bristol, Bradford and other hopeful towns, drawing in the civic dignitaries, retailers and housewives, Rotarians, Soroptomists and even children to special exhibitions, often in museums, to lectures and discussions. They laid on Housewives Forums to which women came demanding squarer saucepans, larger castors and higher three-piece suites. They indoctrinated sales staff with residential conferences, speeches on 'What We Mean by Good Design', and Brains Trusts. They distributed small booklets called 'Four Ways of Living' (dress designer, doctor, chain-store keeper, clerk). They brought out little leaflets saying to the public:

'Design is what makes a thing
   easy to make,
   easy to use,
   easy to look at.'

They sent around their newsheets and analyses of dishracks and pamphlets on 'How to Furnish Your Home', and in 1949 they started to publish large-scale propaganda, *Design* magazine—an act of such confidence, just then, that Francis Meynell, calling it megalomania, resigned.

Design began most tactfully. With just the same soft-pedalling as *Journal of Design* a century before, the first editorial announced that 'This journal begins publication with one purpose, and one purpose only: to help industry in its task of raising standards of design.' With this aim, the first issue included a feature entitled 'Neater Meter' (a before-and-after story), and an article by Gordon Russell asking patiently, for about the hundredth time, 'What is good design?' The answer—a product which is true to its materials, good in appearance and, above all, fit for use— shows how very close the Council's thinking was in those days to the basic pre-war doctrine of the DIA. But the illustrations emphasize a most important difference, something which the DIA had never really tackled. The Beetle plastics sugar dredger shown by Gordon Russell, the strainer and potato masher, proved that with a vengeance the Council was determined not to be too rarified. This was design within the people's ken.

One way and another, by roughly 1950, partly through the Council's efforts, partly independently, design in British industry was visibly improving. Besides the pre-war devotees there were some newer converts. Besides Gordon Russell, there was HK, Race and Hille and Morris of Glasgow. Besides Edinburgh Weavers, there was now Whitehead and Tibor. The pre-war Good Furniture Group had been revived, and a counterpart in Scotland, Scottish Furniture Manufacturers, by then had commissioned new designs. Alongside Heal's and Dunn's, there were many other shops showing sudden post-war interest in modern merchandise: Liberty's in London, Bainbridge's of Newcastle, Hopewells of Nottingham, David Morgan, Cardiff, Hammonds of Hull, Brown's of Newcastle, John Bowler of Brighton. Said *Design* magazine, very pleased, 'The list will grow, for the tide is turning.' It quite definitely was.

In 1946, the *Architectural Review* was grumbling that the daily press, which publicized authors, never mentioned industrial designers. By 1950, *Design* was saying:

'Note the increasing frequency of constructive references to design in the home; see how the women's pages examine the design of household goods; watch the rising demand by editors for hand-picked photographs from the Council of Industrial Design and consider that full page in the Daily Mirror given up to a serious review of *Designers in Britain* under the four-column headline: DESIGN HAS COME INTO YOUR LIFE.'

Surely this deserved a celebration. And in fact, a celebration was underway: an enormous celebration, a national merry-making, a heyday to be known as The Festival of Britain, a grand design bonanza, a sudden burst of glory for the CoID, DIA and even Arts and Crafts. For patriotic Lethaby had said long, long before:

'Nothing better could be thought of as likely to bring real interest back into our towns and villages as some form of Festival.'

154
Utility Furniture Committee
'Chiltern' oak sideboard, 1945.

155
Utility Furniture Committee
'Cotswold' living-room furniture, 1943.

156
Utility Furniture Committee
'Cotswold' dining table, 1943.

157
Utility Furniture Committee
Printed cotton furnishing fabric, 1943.

158
Utility Furniture Committee
'Cotswold' bedroom furniture, 1943.

154

155

156

157

158

159

159
British Army Camouflage Centre
Pneumatic chair developed from
wartime techniques, and shown in
'War to Peace' section, Britain Can
Make It Exhibition, 1946.

160
David Medd
Farmer's bedroom from Britain Can
Make It Exhibition, 1946.

161
R. Y. Goodden
Sports Section from Britain Can
Make It Exhibition, 1946.

160

162

163

164

162
Howard Keith
'Cavalier' chair made by
H.K. Furniture, 1949.

163
Howard Keith
'Intruder' chair made by
H.K. Furniture, 1949.

164
Howard Keith
'Simplon' settee made by
H.K. Furniture, 1948

165
Basil Spence
'Allegro' chair made by H. Morris,
1949.

166
Geoffrey Dunn
Partition shelving and lamp for
Dunn's of Bromley, 1950.

165

166

167

168

167
R. D. Russell
Console television receiver made by Murphy, 1947.

168
Ernest Race
Chairs, table and sideboard made by Race Furniture, between 1946 and 1950.

169
Lucian Ercolani
Windsor chair made by Ercol for Britain Can Make It Exhibition, 1946.

170
Robin Day and Clive Latimer
Storage system, prizewinning design in Low-Cost Furniture Competition, Museum of Modern Art, New York, 1948.

169

171

172

173

174

171
Marian Pepler
'Kelim' woven rug, 1948.

172
Marian Pepler
'Key' tufted rug, 1948.

173
Enid Marx
'Skelda' upholstery fabric, designed
for Utility Furniture Committee
1945.

174
Enid Marx
Woven fabric, designed for
Utility Furniture Committee 1946.

175
Enid Marx
'Ring' cotton tapestry, designed for
Utility Furniture Committee, 1945.

175

176

176
Margaret Leischner
Woven fabric, 1945–50.

177
Margaret Leischner
Woven fabric, 1945–50.

177

178

179

180

178
Sheila Pickersgill
Hand-printed linen, 1949.

179
Tibor Reich
Woven furnishing fabric, early
post-war.

180
Tibor Reich
Woven furnishing fabric, early
post-war.

181

181
Gaby Schreiber
Stacking cups in plastic, 1946.

182
Susie Cooper
'Spiral Fern' earthenware, 1940–41.

183
Susie Cooper
'Laurel Border' hand-painted
earthenware, 1935.

184
A. B. Read
'Versalite' table lamp made by
Troughton and Young, about 1945.

185
John Waterer
'Oxford' leather zipper bags made
by S. Clarke, about 1947.

183

184

185

6

The Industrial Designers 1951-1960

HUDDLED in a cubby hole, a former footman's bedroom, in one of those imperious red houses behind Harrods, Hugh Casson and his Festival Design Group apprehensively sat hour after hour sipping Bisodol and wondering how ever they could make an exhibition on their badly-blitzed and desolate, depressing South Bank site.

The idea of the Festival was mooted some years earlier: incongruously enough, in the middle of the War, the Royal Society of Arts had proposed a 1951 exhibition to commemorate Prince Albert's glorious outburst a hundred years before. This private suggestion was reinforced more publicly in 1945 when John Gloag, voice of the DIA resurgent, wrote to *The Times*, and almost simultaneously Gerald Barry, then editor of the *News Chronicle*, published an Open Letter to Sir Stafford Cripps. What they both wanted was an international exhibition, and as it turned out, they hardly need have asked. For Cripps, an exhibition enthusiast who had built 'Britain Can Make It' almost singlehanded, was already making plans for a festival in Britain. He sent one of his urgent red-ink letters back to Barry, expressing his sympathy; within another fortnight, the Ramsden Committee was set up, which recommended 'a first category international exhibition,' held at the earliest practicable date, 'to demonstrate to the world the recovery of the United Kingdom from the effects of the war in the moral, cultural, spiritual and material fields'.

This was 1946. By the time it reached Hugh Casson, three years later, the Festival of Britain was not so grandiose. By then it was not international, just British; the country's economics, lack of housing, loss of factories, had cut down the plans to a more manageable size, reducing the theme from universal showmanship to national reassessment. The Festival would now be a national morale-booster, a time for fun and fantasy; after a decade of war, deprivation and darkness, it was to be a moment of remembrance of things past and incentive to things future. In this heady atmosphere, the organizers were directed to display 'the British contribution to civilization, past, present and future, in the arts, in science and technology, and in industrial design'. Stafford Cripps, the President of the Board of Trade, had handed on the Festival—which was no longer tradesmanlike—to the Lord President of the Council, Herbert Morrison. The Festival Council had been appointed. Under Gerald Barry, by then (what fitter person?) Director-General of all festivities, the Festival Executive Committee was at work; and under the Committee was the Presentation Panel, and then beneath the Panel was Hugh Casson's Design Unit, appointed to give shape to the patriotic concept, to bring the fun and fantasy alive beside the Thames.

'They enjoyed it,' said Hugh Casson on the BBC, talking to the Schools in 1951, 'they laughed a lot and from the very beginning they made up their minds that it shouldn't be pompous or boring.'

He and James Holland, James Gardner, Ralph Tubbs and Misha Black sat shivering in overcoats for hours, day after day, in the attic room in Knightsbridge with drawing boards on their knees and tracing paper piling up around them, determined that the Festival should be bright, gay and popular and totally inspiring on its awkward tiny site. No long palatial vistas, but small ones, interlocking; no ponderous pavilions, but buildings grouped informally: Hugh Casson described it, to the Schools and Olive Shapley (who was trilling with excitement), as a very large house with the roof taken off and the pavilions laid out like outdoor rooms.

Who was to design the various Pavilions and Restaurants and showpieces? Hugh Casson and his Unit needed men of genius, but as time was short, they could not afford men of temperament. They settled, very wisely, for themselves and many friends: Black and Holland on the Upstream Circuit, 'The Land'; James Gardner on the Downstream Circuit, 'The People'; Ralph Tubbs on the Dome of Discovery—provided that the Dome could in fact be fitted in. ('It seemed doubtful,' said Casson, 'because in a fit of exhibitionism we had decided it must be 365 feet across and we clung to that dimension with pathetic assurance.') The Lion and the Unicorn Pavilion was assigned to Robert Goodden and Dick Russell; Homes and Gardens to Katz & Vaughan; the Tele cinema to Wells Coates; the Shot Tower to Casson and Gardner. The teamwork was quite breathtaking for Britain—a country where up to then team spirit in design was non-existent—extending to the litter bins (Jack Howe) and chairs (by Race) and signposts (by Milner Gray and Robin Day). A hundred or more designers were employed. There was somebody responsible for every little detail, the ice-cream stalls and flower-pots, the sculpture and the murals, the knives and forks and pottery, the bird boxes and even the breed of ducks selected for the ornamental lake.

The Council of Industrial Design was much involved; the Council and the Festival seemed made for one another. The Council was the source of all the manufactured objects; the Festival the carrot (or the stick) for manufacturers, urging them to try a little harder with design. The original scheme had been for a pavilion, a separate pavilion, of industrial design, but Gordon Russell who argued—much like Morris—that design is all around us, resisted the idea of a Good Design Pavilion. Fearing clumsy WCs and basins in the public lavatories, unco-ordinated lettering, badly-chosen chairs and a general lack of function throughout the Festival, he suggested that his Council, far from being confined to one exemplary pavilion, should oversee the lot. The rule was made that nothing in industrial production should be included without CoID approval, thus eliminating free-for-all Halls of Textiles, Pavilions of Confectionery, Palaces of Gas: there were to be no Winston Churchills in Swiss roll, no effigies of royalty in edible fats; a paper manufacturers' proposal to exhibit a model of the South Bank in lavatory paper was regretfully declined. 'No stunts,' said Gordon Russell to his industrial officers before he sent them out to gather British products: 'They will be real goods to go into real shops and so be available for real people. This may not be an earth-shattering statement, but it is British common sense.'

Sensibly, the Council thought up and implemented the 1951 Stock List, a card-index of all the well-designed articles the officers could search out in a systematic survey of the industries, from locomotives to henhouses, from tableware to sailing boats, all organized so neatly in 70 categories that finally the Stock List was itself exhibited, renamed (more festively perhaps) 'Design Review'. Doggedly, the Council persuaded twenty-eight British manufacturers to work for eighteen months in the Festival Pattern Group, decorating products with patterns derived from crystal structure diagrams, taking advice from a scientist at Girton, triumphantly producing dress-prints based on haemoglobin, crystal-structure curtain fabrics, plastic sheets and ties, crystal-structure lighting fittings, dinner plates and wine-glasses, a crystal-structure foyer for the Science Exhibition. Sir Lawrence Bragg politely wrote to say how pleased he was. The *Architectural Review* was not so keen. It is certain that the project, mingling art and science and industry, would have been dear to the heart of Henry Cole.

Cole would have approved of the whole conduct of the Council at the Festival of Britain: its calmness and efficiency; the way (against all odds) it organized the loan of a large locomotive from Glasgow; the way in which it collected, stored and catalogued and finally returned 10,000 objects from 3,500 firms—an operation managed by Benoy, a retired major-general, whose experience with moving troops for the African invasion in World War II stood him in good stead. Best of all, the Council had succeeded in not ruffling, and not being ruffled by, industry too much. The standards of selection were deliberately moderate. Wrote Gordon Russell in The *Architectural Review* (which had complained, as usual, about the Council's leniency):

'Our aim was to find something worth showing from the greatest number of firms possible, otherwise we should run the risk of all the exhibits in certain trades coming from three or four firms, which could hardly be tolerated in an operation financed by public funds on this scale.'

Perhaps it was this moderation, the discovery that modern design was, after all, approachable; perhaps it was the fact that the Festival was billed as 'the people's show, not organized arbitrarily for them to enjoy, but put on largely by them, by us all, as an expression of a way of life in which we believe'; perhaps it was the intoxication of the time when Churchill, in medals, rode up the escalator in the Dome of Discovery and everybody cheered and danced in the open-air along the Fairway and set off in balloons for unknown destinations; perhaps it was the brilliance of Casson's small piazzas and pretty outdoor cafés and the cat-walk and the Skylon; perhaps it was the crystals which the purists so despised: whatever the reason, or accumulated reasons, modern design seemed suddenly all right. The public, which had for a century resisted all benevolent attempts to bring them good design—from Prince Albert's workmen's cottages of 1851, the 1905 Cheap Cottages at Letchworth, the display of 'Industrial Art for the Slender Purse' in 1929 at the Victoria and Albert, the DIA pre-war working-class showhouses, 'Homes for the People' in Manchester in wartime, Pick's well-intentioned survey of 'The Working-Class Home' (about which they cared nothing)—over-night came round. They went off in their thousands to the show-house at Lansbury furnished entirely, with CoID approval, for £143 4s 7d; where Bill, a dock-worker, his wife Mary (35) who had been in service and understood good housekeeping, their children, Jack, Jill, Jane and Baby Tom (4–5 months) lived happily with blue distemper walls and dark blue paper, starred and dotted, on the wall above the chimney, an extending dining table, an expanding coffee table, a reversible trolley convertible to card-table, 'Jack and Jill' easy chairs, a brass-stem standard lamp and russet wild-flower curtains (7s 11d a yard).

Gerald Barry had insisted that 1951 must be something more than a year of bigger and better exhibitions and more and merrier festivals; his idea that the Festival should be a sort of springboard for young architects and artists and designers had in fact come beautifully true. Neville Ward, for instance, wrote that 'Ward and Austin were (just) in practice, two of the three of us still in our twenties; so to be invited to take part in the South Bank project was wonderful. It was, in a time of few and small opportunities, a big thing.' The repercussions, both for design and for designers, are still not really over—nearly twenty years beyond. The Casson-Black contingent went from strength to strength; the Royal College of Art was greatly glorified by the contributions of its practising professors, and the students on the fringe of its absorbed the optimism and understood the discipline and teamwork of it all. The British began paying more attention to detail: to good letter-ing on captions and on signposts, to interior and exterior furniture, electrical fitments, litter-bins and landscaping, to texture and the colour of paving and to lighting, things which they had hardly bothered with before. Individual objects, which were first seen on the South Bank, ranging from Race bright steel-rod chairs to concrete flower bowls, were soon found far and wide. Barry, who saw everything, summed it up quite wisely: 'In this bold use of colour, in the marriage of architecture and sculpture, in scrupulous use of landscaping, in attention to elegance and finish in interior and exterior fittings, new standards and a new style were set up—the 'Festival Style'—which evidently caught the imagination of other designers and also created a public or commercial *demand*. It was copied all over the country—copied, and gradually debased. In due course the Festival style became a cliché. Probably this was inevitable.'

Making the most of Festivaliana, of course, was Gordon Russell with his Council lined behind him. This was their great moment, in the national excitement, in the year in which a public outcry had demolished a Tudor refreshment car thought up by British Railways, to consolidate for ever the movement for reform, to try once and for all to break down the vicious circle which for ages had prevented real progress in design. They kept 'Design Review', the Stock List from the Festival; by then they had accumulated rather more good-will from the manufacturers; contemporary case-histories prove time and time again, unlikely as it seems, that manufacturers whose products were rejected had afterwards come to the Council for advice. In the greatly improved climate of the fifties, a system—simple in outline, elaborate in operation—was developed, and soon became the envy of, and model for, reformers of design in other European countries. (It was not very long before Muthesius walked again.)

What happened, and still happens, was this, in briefest outline. The CoID might suggest to a British manufacturer that one (or maybe all) of his designs could be improved on. The manufacturer might then come back to the Council for the names of some designers with the relevant experience. A designer might be chosen to work with the manufacturer (on staff or freelance basis) to produce a new design, which might then be submitted to the Council for approval, which might then be accepted for 'Design Review', exhibited to retailers, shown to the public in the various design centres, ultimately—in the most ideal conditions—winning a Design Centre Award.

This may sound cut-and-dried, but the system evolved slowly. It took years for the Council to make its purpose known, and years to gain enough support for tangible achievement. Through the early fifties, the scale of operations (compared with that in 1962 or 1963) was small. In 1953, the Record of Designers had only 350 requests from manufacturers; and one must remember that the Haymarket Design Centre was not in fact opened until 1956, and Design Centre Awards did not in fact begin until 1957. But onwards from the Festival, the system was immeasurably strengthened by designers trained to be designers, from the RCA and other colleges of art. This was one large reason for the Council's rush of confidence; the training of designers at long last seemed secure. It was 1951 when the Des. RCA was first awarded to students completing the design course at the Royal College of Art (in addition to 9 months' experience in industry). In 1952, the students held an exhibition on Liberty's Fourth Floor and RCA designers' names, which later appeared almost ad nauseam, were for the first time listed in *Design* magazine: for instance, Ronald Carter, Eric Clements, Gerald Benney, David Mellor, Robert Jefferson; Frank Guille designed a cot for Prince Charles and Philip Popham made intricate medallions for decorating it. The next year, *Design* reported favourably on the students' exhibition in the Victoria and Albert Museum: this time Alan Irvine, with two chairs and a razor-case, and Geoffrey Baxter's glass designs emerged with honour, and Pat Albeck was reported to have sold a design of fruit in green and yellow on cambric to Horrockses. By 1953, the RCA reported that out of the 59 students who had left, 44 had posts in industry. By 1957, *Designers in Britain* (the SIA catalogue) showed Des. RCA products on every other page: Guille's designs for Kandya, Robert Welch's stainless steel for Wiggin, David Mellor's cutlery for Walker & Hall, Robert Heritage's furniture for Evans. Also in the issue was a certain Terence Conran (though he was at the Central School and not the RCA) with a picture of an unusually long sideboard produced by Conran Furniture, more or less home-made.

A new kind of designer was emerging: not architect, not artist and not exactly craftsman, British but not necessarily a gentleman, a well-trained and ambitious young self-made one-man show. The scale of operations in America, where offices were sometimes 50-strong, seemed most unsympathetic to students who were trained in knowledge of materials and personal experiment. The Scandinavian system of individual offices seemed rather more ideal, and many of the students, from the RCA especially, set up on their own as designers straightaway, with a faith, enthusiasm and love and care for detail which had not been seen in Britain since the days of Arts and Crafts. For instance: the RCA-trained furniture designers Ronald Carter and Robert Heritage; the textile designers Audrey Levy, Pat Albeck, Shirley Craven; the jeweller John Donald; the silversmith/industrial designers Gerald Benney, Robert Welch and David Mellor. Robert Welch, in Chipping Campden, opened his own workshop in Ashbee's old headquarters; in Sheffield, David Mellor set up his own office and metal-working shop. The difference, of course, was that whereas C. R. Ashbee and his craftsmen worked mostly on special commissions, Robert Welch and David Mellor, besides their one-off silver, used their workshops for production of industrial prototypes: alongside special silver for Churchill College, Cambridge, Robert Welch would be working on designs for stainless steel; as well as a cross for Southwell Minster, David Mellor would design a cast-iron heater or a lamp-post or a litter-bin. In Britain in the fifties a new realistic breed of designers was evolving a new realistic style: or, in point of fact, developing traditional

British virtues of common sense and wholesomeness, simplicity and reticence, designer's lack of pomp and craftsman's truth to his materials, into a good, decent, measured, modest, modern style.

Decency, just then, was meat and drink to the Council of Industrial Design, which in 1953 had made the sound announcement that

'Though rules of thumb and narrow definitions are neither feasible nor desirable, the general principle can be stated that the object of the Council's selections is to promote good design as comprising good materials and workmanship, fitness for purpose and pleasure in use.'

This was the principle of all its activities: its bulletins and lectures, its photographic library, its visual aids for schools, its travelling exhibitions. It was clearly to be seen in the illustrations chosen for the Annual Reports: the office dictaphone, the pickled beetroot label, the dress-shield display dispenser, all shown in 1953, along with the unit bedroom furniture designed by Frank Austin, 'as a result of the meeting between CoID staff and the firm's managing director'. Goodness and fitness and pleasure were all obvious in the CoID show-flats and show-houses round the country, and the CoID Ideal Home displays of decent living, with Ward & Austin pianos, and shelves by Robert Heritage, Stag wardrobes designed by John and Sylvia Reid, Kandya chairs, Reynolds Woodware sideboards and Conelamps, adjustable and washable and pleated, clean and neat in acetate, by Cooke-Yarborough and Homes.

A pleasant time it was, when standards seemed so certain, and good design meant comeliness and usefulness and sense, and the London Design Centre was opened by the Duke of Edinburgh who wished it the very best of luck. It had taken so long coming— back in 1931 Gorell and his committee had stressed the crying need for a central exhibition, and committees ever after had demanded and demanded a Pavilion of Design—that once the Centre opened in 1956, thanks to Walter Worboys, CoID Chairman, thanks to Gordon Russell's indefatigable spadework, and thanks to £27,000 from industry, it seemed a great occasion. DIA prayers seemed answered. Here at last in London was a showplace for design. What if Buckminster Fuller called it 'Bargain basement stuff; you're designing for today in the idiom of ten years ago'; and what if Charles Eames, visiting the Centre, found it 'very creepy'. Mr Gaitskell and his wife had said that they wished they had seen the Centre earlier, before they had altered their Hampstead home, and Marghanita Laski had felt that 'any woman who is at all interested in good design will feel an immense debt of gratitude to the CoID for starting the Centre'. The *Daily Telegraph* even predicted it might make us the best-furnished nation in the world.

So on with honest business: selection committees on Tuesdays and on Thursdays to assess the various products submitted to the Council. A group of outside specialists, designers, architects and retailers, backed up by Council members and CoID staff, sat in judgement on up to 200 products, regaled at 3 o'clock by a cup of Council tea, asking, in general, the old DIA questions on fitness for purpose and pleasure in use. Will it pour or cut or hold things? Is it man-size, child-size, ship-shape? Is it functional and proper? Is it fair and square and good, performing (when it needs to) reasonable ablutions? Provided that the judges, heirs of Ambrose Heal, were satisfied, the product could then (on payment of a fee) be shown in the Design Centre and (if the manufacturers wrote in for special labels) could be emblazoned 'Design Centre Approved'.

Ten years before, such a scheme would not have worked: British manufacturers would not have dreamed of paying for space in a selective exhibition of design. Though even now some grumbled and fumed about the Council and its ignorant committees and its high-falutin' principles, the fact that every day 2,000 people came to see the exhibition in the Haymarket bore weight. Bit by bit, by conferences, with a Scottish Design Centre (under Alister Maynard, the furniture designer and one-time ADC to the Governor of Bengal), with Design Centres attached to Building Centres in the provinces, the cause of good design was patiently argued and precisely illustrated. By tactful, careful conduct, by general efficiency, by constantly opposing the idea of long-haired art, the Council showed the manufacturers that there was nothing so extreme about its policy. The level of selection remained thoroughly Home Service, design for a large public, the aesthetic middlebrow.

What is interesting is that, in spite of all this tolerance, the Council was then, in a sense, quite narrow-minded. This, again, was a great strength: through the early and mid-fifties, Gordon Russell was almost exclusively intent on raising design standards in consumer industries. No dallying, at this stage, with design in engineering; no veering off to contemplate the face of the land, few thoughts about environment and mass-communications. For the moment, the main aim was better teacups, chairs and tables. 'Limited advance and consolidate', his motto, reached its point of glory with Design Centre Awards. In 1957, two RCA Professors (Goodden and Russell), Brian O'Rorke the architect, Milner Gray, Master of the Faculty of Royal Designers for Industry, and Mrs Astrid Sampe, picked out twelve outstandingly simple and practical objects: dinner and teaware, table glasses, wallpaper, cutlery, a curtain fabric, a carpet, plastic tableware, a lamp shade, a TV set, a convertible settee-bed, Pyrex casseroles and a convector open fire.

'Although,' wrote the judges, on a note of some surprise, 'none of the articles selected was chosen for its affinity with another, in the case of the table glass, dinner ware and cutlery it is interesting to see in the result how well the selected examples would combine as a place setting.' Interesting certainly; but surely not surprising. It was thoroughly predictable—might one say inevitable?— given the Council's emphasis on clean appearance, sound workmanship and suitability for purpose, that Design Centre Awards would tend to look alike. They were in a sense the Council's own great prizes. They pointed out, discreetly, what the Council had achieved.

For 1957 Awards and the prizes given on each successive year (with the bonus of the Duke of Edinburgh's Prize for Elegant Design) brought extraordinary glory to the partnerships beginning to build up between the freelance designer and his clients. Year after year, design awards were given (or seemed to be given) to Robin Day and Hille, the Reids and Rotaflex, Hulme Chadwick and Wilkinson Sword, Humphrey Spender and Edinburgh Weavers, Audrey Levy and Wall Paper Manufacturers, Edward Pond and Bernard Wardle, Robert Welch and Old Hall, Robert Heritage and Archie Shine, and David Mellor and Walker & Hall. Year after year—and this was no illusion—design awards became an accolade for Royal College of Art training. Robin Darwin wrote a letter to *Design* magazine in 1958 pointing out that 35 per cent of the 20 'Designs of the Year' was the work of designers who had studied at the RCA during the previous seven years. Besides—he added, to be fair—'two other winning designers belong to an earlier generation'.

Design was still in many ways an amiable clique. Identical professors seemed forever giving prizes to their own RCA students, identical designers were forever smiling thanks to the Duke of Edinburgh. The DIA still talked of 'spreading the gospel', and for that very purpose held house-parties at Ashridge, gentle country gatherings they called 'Design Weekends'. The fact was that the Council of Industrial Design had stolen the DIA's thunder; through the fifties, its activities were altogether cosy and low-key, with lunch meetings at Overseas House (sample topic: *Design Starvation in the Public Schools*); with musical evenings in the Geffrye Museum; with little exhibitions in Charing Cross Station, 'Register Your Choice' and later 'Make or Mar'. In the course of these meanderings, all leisurely and friendly, the only thing which seemed to rouse the DIA to fury was the fashionable, frivolous, dreadfully unreasonable, totally un-functional stiletto heel. In 1959, Lord Conesford, the President, clinging as if to a lifebelt to the principle that 'Fitness for purpose is the very essence of good design', launched an attack as furious as any of the thunderings of Gloag:

'A woman wearing such shoes does far more destruction to the floor of an aeroplane in which she travels than a wild rhinoceros, which can be transported without doing any damage at all.'

And yet, in spite of the family circle of DIA and RCA and CoID, in spite of the assumption that design was still the gospel to be spread to unbelievers, unseen by some old preachers there was by now a change. Hamilton Temple Smith, by then the oldest, had noticed it as early as 1951: 'The heathen,' he wrote, 'no longer stone us out of their cities: they are more likely to offer us a cocktail. And this frightens me.' Marghanita Laski had noticed it, and rather to the horror of the courteous DIA, stated in the *Year Book* 'The day of the design we have fought and struggled for these many years is already over. It is popular, accepted and boring.' In a way, she was right: from the Festival onwards design —or Design as it became—was all around. Design was on the railways: in 1956, British Railways Design Panel was hopefully established. (George Williams, the first Design Director, had been on the staff of the CoID.) Design had reached the Ministry of Works, where Harold Glover, the Controller of Supplies, persistently raised standards. The LCC Architects Department, in particular the Furniture Section directed by Frank Height, designed official furniture for LCC schools, colleges, offices and welfare homes, controlling all the colours for all LCC buildings. The Ministry of Transport offered what amounted to bribes for good design, subsidizing lighting on trunk roads on condition that local authorities selected lighting columns already approved by the CoID. Meanwhile Ernest Marples, the new Postmaster General, announced a design policy which, if it had matured, might have towered above the rest: he would modernize the Post Offices, posters, greetings telegrams; redesign the telephone kiosks and consider new telephones. Mr Marples himself would test all the mock-ups; he would listen to advice but he would not always take it.

This was the age in which Design became a factor in public image-building. Successive PMGs promised the public better-designed pillar-boxes; managing directors of forward-looking companies commissioned themselves symbols and new, dynamic letter-headings. Corporate identity programmes began flourishing on airlines, in laundries, in off-licences, in banks. The reformers' age-old plans for uniting art and commerce had at last materialized, not quite as they imagined. Design was advertising; Design was serious commerce; Design was the concern of Boards of Directors, a development acknowledged with characteristic pomp by the Royal Society of Arts which from 1954, the year of its Bicentenary, awarded (and awards) annual medals to people who 'in a manner other than as industrial designers have exerted an exceptional influence in promoting art and design in British industry'. The first four medals went to good artistic businessmen: 1954 Sir Colin Anderson, 1955 Sir Charles Tennyson, 1956 Sir Walter Worboys and 1957 Sir Ernest Goodale.

This was the era of management consultants: design consultants fitted neatly in beside them. This was the beginning of consumer-dom: Design of course, appealed strongly to readers of *'Which?'*. This was the age of 'Outrage' and the Anti-Ugly demonstrations when people shouted 'Hell' and beat drums and carried coffins to appalling modern buildings: Design (and William Morris' ghost) was here as well. Design was in the shops and Design was in the showrooms, the posters and advertisements. Design was on TV: 'Design Review' became a monthly woman's feature, introducing Moira Hallifax of Peter Jones, Sloane Square. Design was, most of all, on the bookstalls. A vast factor in promotion of Design were the magazines, from prestigious *Ambassador* (the export publication munificently managed by Hans and Elspeth Juda) to the mass-circulation monthlies and weeklies for the housewife by the fireside. Home editors were born.

In 1953, at Coronation time, *Ideal Home* made the rousing, very patriotic statement that 'The finest efforts of living designers, encouraged by everyone's desire for the best, will safeguard our heritage.' In fact this was a turning point. The work of living designers—up to then a specialist subject for *Design* magazine, the *Architectural Review* and esoteric foreign publications, like *Mobilia*, *Graphis*, *Domus*—was featured in more general, domestic magazines. In 1953, *Ideal Home* was running features on 'Silver in the Home', showing RCA silversmiths; 'At Home with the Days', showing Lucienne and Robin chatting in their studio; a genial and encouraging lecture by Paul Reilly called 'Don't be Afraid of Contemporary Design'.

'Our hearts and Heal's,' wrote Diana Pollock, who joined the magazine in 1956, 'obviously beat as one although we often have to present a different picture (like any other form of communication we have our potential and our limitations).' Mrs Pollock, first and most determined of Home Editors, concocted Ideal Home Commissioned Designs, a true project of the fifties—brave, consumer-minded, very sound yet mildly gay. She found gaps in the market 'created by the new social climate'; she found the young designers equipped to fill these gaps; she found the manufacturers to try out the ideas, with guaranteed publicity. She then arranged the meeting between the manufacturer and the designer, with the editor of *Ideal Home* in the chair. The results of this benevolence ranged from Mozart pianos to saucepan-lid racks, from multi-glide storage to heated trolleys, from matching p.v.c. curtaining and Con-tact to 'Plantagon', a decorative unit flower-pot. 'Form' seating system, designed by Robin Day, went on to win a Design Centre Award.

Home and *Homes and Gardens*, *House Beautiful* and *Housewife*, *Everywoman*, *Woman and Home* and *Woman's Journal*: within the next few years, the homely magazines enlarged and multiplied. In *Woman*, the most basic, Edith Blair (alias Norah Schlegel, another editor whose heart beat much like Heal's and a DIA subscriber) with extraordinary patience watered down Design for a mass-readership, using orange on the walls in 1957, in 1958 recommending lilac blue with coffee and cream and by 1961 suggesting dark brown paint with jewel colours in the furnishing. Meanwhile *House and Garden, Vogue*'s domestic counterpart, most superior and cleverest of housebound magazines, was promoting a whole range of *House and Garden* colours—forest green and cardinal red, middy blue, light gunmetal and other urbane shades—and Olive Sullivan, the Decoration Editor, was evolving, in her room sets, an influential style, fresh, clean and pseudo-countrified, elaborate and charming, combining fine new pieces with a nice accumulation of well-picked bric-a-brac.

As fervent propagandists for design the journalists were considerably fiercer than the CoID. On factory tours, immaculate small parties of lady journalists in smart imposing hats would tackle manufacturers, who generally seemed dumbfounded, and ask them why their standards of design were mediocre. Why cut that glass decanter when it looks much better plainer? Why paint that cup with roses when it looks so lovely white? Why not treat designers the way they do in Sweden? Why not be like Gustavsberg, Arabia or Orrefors? For this was the time when Scandinavia, to the journalists and other tasteful people, approximated heaven.

To encourage them, Paul Stemann at Finmar was importing Wegner chairs and Gense stainless steel, Arabia pottery and Kaare Klint paper lampshades which RCA designers seemed to buy in bulk. The Green Group (the Good Furnishing Group of retailers in a new and more Nordic incarnation) was importing substantial quantities of Scandinavian furniture. Little shops, craft-orientated, Scandinavian in tenor, with a comfortable love of well-made little things, now appeared in Britain: the first was Primavera, Henry Rothschild's shop in Sloane Street in 1945, and by the later fifties they were opening in dozens. In Sheffield, Interior Decorations; in Manchester, Malcolm Bishop; in Doncaster and Retford, York Tenn, Yorkshire design shops apparently directly inspired by Scandinavia, based on the Swedish design shop, Svensk Tenn. And everywhere you went, you were almost sure of finding a Svensk or Norsk or Dansk shop, full of stainless steel and teak.

This love of Scandinavia was at its most fastidious in the upper reaches of the RCA, in the Western Galleries, the long dank College workshops above the Aeronautical Museum. On top of Wilbur Wright and his experimental aeroplane, Professor R. D. Russell and David Pye were teaching their furniture students to respect the plain and simple, to understand construction, to care for natural wood, to appreciate the Swedish understatement of Carl Malmsten, to worship the finesse of the Danish school of Klint: Scandinavian designers who were, in their turn, indebted to the British eighteenth-century fine sturdy craftsman style.

Design had gone full circle; the British avant-garde was in-fluenced by Denmark which was influenced by Britain. At the same time, more directly, the British craft tradition revived by Webb and Gimson in the later nineteenth century began to be appreciated. Morris and his friends, up to now the rather private preserve of *Architectural Review* readers and Pevsner, were revealed in all their beauty and virility and Britishness, their quaintness and their honesty, for all the world to see. For the Festival of Britain 'The Cotswold Tradition' was exhibited in Cheltenham by Oliver Hill, showing Ashbee and Gimson and the Barnsleys in their setting of patient Cotswold building and sheep-shearing and hay-making. The next year Peter Floud, Keeper of Circulation at the Victoria and Albert Museum, an addict of the period, put on an exhibition of 'Victorian and Edwardian Decorative Arts', showing Godwin, showing Dresser, showing central Arts and Crafts, and offshoots as far-flung as Peasant Industries in Hasle-mere. An era which had seemed almost wholly unimportant, of negligible interest if not an outright joke, seemed suddenly quite vital. Voysey was a hero; and people began noticing Charles Rennie Mackintosh.

In 1959, Gordon Russell, a designer with the Cotswold tradi-tion very much at heart, a philosopher in tune with Gimson and with Ashbee, the British modern movement in a way personified, retired from the Council of Industrial Design. By then he had been knighted and the Queen, as she had tapped him gently on the shoulder with the sword, had kindly murmured a few words on the success of the CoID, and—wrote Sir Gordon—'I felt gratified that her reaction, as usual, would be that of a great many of her subjects.' In 1959, the Council was awarded the Gran Premio Internazionale la Rinascente Compasso d'Oro, recognition from Milan 'as the oldest and most efficient government organiza-tion for the development and popularization of good design'. Calling himself the Council's scheduled ancient monument, feasted and presented with an English oak staircase by the CoID members, and a tankard from the Arts Club, and an old cut-glass decanter from the Scottish Committee, Gordon Russell went his way, back to Kingcombe in the Cotswolds, and soon the entire character of British design changed.

186
Robert and Roger Nicholson
Dining recess from Homes and Gardens Pavilion, Festival of Britain, 1951.

187
Robert and Roger Nicholson
Sitting room for an old lady from Homes and Gardens Pavilion, 1951.

188
Ernest Race
'Springbok' chairs made by Race Furniture, on South Bank, 1951.

189
K. G. Browne
Unicorn restaurant sign, 1951.

190
Robert Sevant
Festival Pattern Group wallpaper derived from crystal structure diagram of insulin, made by John Line, 1951.

188

189   190

191
Ernest Race
'Antelope' chair made by Race
Furniture, 1950.

192
Ernest Race
'Cormorant' deck chair made by
Race Furniture, on board the
Oriana, 1955.

193
Ernest Race
'Flamingo' chair made by Race
Furniture, 1956.

194
Howard Keith
'Eloquence' easy chair made by
H.K. Furniture, 1952.

195
Robin Day
'Hillestak' chair in moulded plywood
made by Hille, 1951.

196
Booth and Ledeboer
Mahogany sideboard with recessed
rosewood door fronts made by
Gordon Russell Furniture, 1951.

194

195

196

197
Ward and Austin
Bedroom furniture made by
Loughborough, 1955.

198
Ward and Austin
Bedroom furniture made by
Loughborough, 1957.

199
Robin Day
Convertible bed settee made by
Hille, 1957.

200
Robin Day
'Form' unit seating made by Hille,
1957.

201

202

203

201
Robert Heritage
Storage unit made by G. W. Evans,
1952.

202
Robin Day
Television receiver made by Pye,
1957.

203
Robert Heritage
'Hamilton' sideboard made by
Archie Shine, 1958.

204
John and Sylvia Reid
Dining-room furniture in teak made
by Stag, 1959.

205
George Fejer and Eric Pamphilon
'Manhattan' chairs and settee made
by Guy Rogers, 1958–9.

204

205

206

207

208

206
Marian Mahler
Printed fabric made by David
Whitehead, late 1940s.

207
Marian Mahler
Printed fabric made by David
Whitehead, late 1940s.

208
Jacqueline Groag
Printed fabric made by David
Whitehead, late 1940s.

209
Lucienne Day
'Calyx' printed cotton made by
Heal Fabrics, 1951.

210
Lucienne Day
'Fothergay' linen glass cloths made
by Thomas Somerset, 1960.

209

210

211

212

213

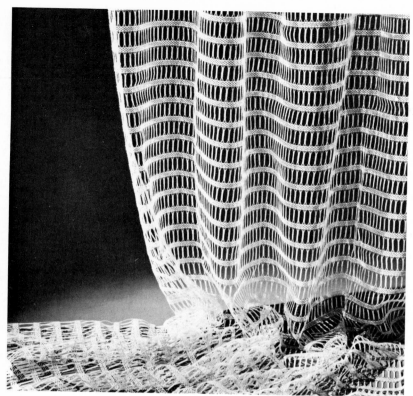

211
Humphrey Spender
'Inglewood' cotton/rayon furnishing fabric made by Edinburgh Weavers, 1959.

212
Tibor Reich
Furnishing fabric, mid-1950s.

213
Ronald Grierson
'Regatta' carpet made by Stockwell, 1953.

214
F. G. Hobden
'Vision Net' in cotton/terylene made by Clyde Manufacturing Co., 1958.

215
Audrey Tanner
'Mandala' Wilton carpet made by Carpet Manufacturing Co., 1959.

214

216
Susie Cooper
'Whispery Grass' china, 1956.

217
Edward Bawden
'Heartsease' muffin dish and teaset
made by Wedgwood for Orient Line,
1952.

218
Robert Stewart
Kitchen storage jars in earthenware,
1959.

218

219

220

219
R. Stennett-Willson
'Tower' table glass made by
Nazeing Glassworks for Wilmart,
1959.

220
*Milner Gray with Kenneth Lamble
and John Cochrane of Design Research
Unit*
Part of a range of Pyrex oven-to-
table glassware made by James
Jobling, 1955–65.

221
Noel London and Howard Upjohn
'Chef Royal' enamelled steel
saucepans made by Edward Curran,
1960.

222

223

224

222
Robert Welch
Stainless steel jugs made by Old Hall, 1958.

223
Robert Welch
Silver coffee urn made for Churchill College, Cambridge, 1960.

224
David Mellor
'Pride' silver teaset made by Walker and Hall, 1958.

225
Robert Welch
Stainless steel toast rack made by Old Hall, 1955.

226
David Mellor
'Pride' silver cutlery made by Walker and Hall, 1954.

225

227

227
E. Cooke-Yarborough and Ronald Homes
Electric light fitting made by
Conelight, 1954.

228
D. W. Morphy
Electric iron made by Morphy-
Richards, 1952.

229
C. W. F. Longman
'Packaway' refrigerator made by
Prestcold Division of Pressed Steel,
1959.

230
Jack Howe
Electric wall clock made by Gent,
1956.

231
David Ogle
'Rayburn' convector fire made by
Allied Ironfounders, 1957.

228

229

230

232
R. David Carter
'Orbit' castor made by J. Gillott, 1961.

233
John Waterer
Coach hide case for typewriter made
by S. Clarke for British Olivetti, 1951.

234
Hulme Chadwick
Pruner made by Wilkinson Sword, 1956.

232

231

233   234

235
Christian Barman
Bus stop for London Transport, 1959.

236
Richard Stevens
Street lighting column made for
Atlas Lighting, 1959.

237
Neville Conder
Telephone kiosk designed for G.P.O.,
1958.

238
Douglas Scott
'Pay-on-Answer' telephone coin box
designed for G.P.O., 1955–7.

239
Jack Howe
Transport shelter in timber designed
for London Transport, 1954.

235   236

237

238

239

7
Union Jacks and the Computer
1960-1969

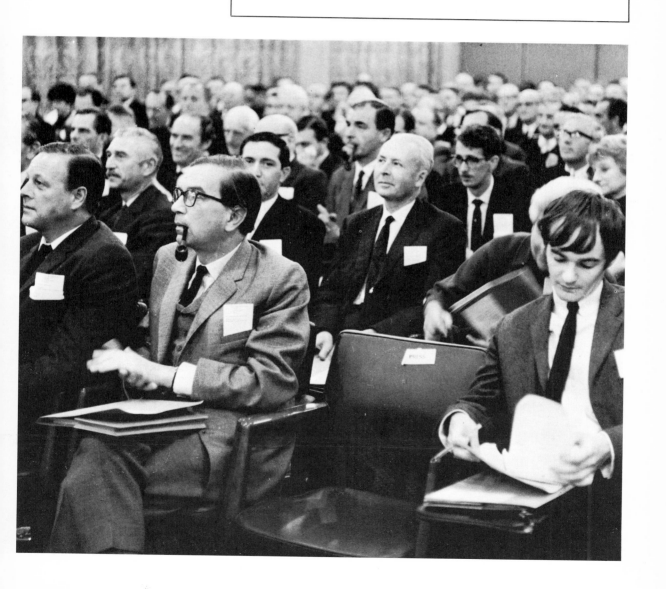

'The Princess Margaret, Countess of Snowdon and
The Earl of Snowdon this evening visited an
Exhibition of Perspex at the Royal College of Art.'

THIS was the announcement from Kensington Palace, published
in *The Times* Court Circular and showing how far the royal spirit
of patronage had moved from Prince Albert's workmen's cottages,
the Duchess of York's poker-work, Prince Edward's functional
reading lamp of 1933, and even the Duke of Edinburgh's Prize for
Elegant Design, first awarded in 1959. For in the 1960s, in Lord
Snowdon, a professional photographer and film-maker, designer
of an aluminium Aviary for London Zoo, reformers of design had
a most practical supporter—more convincing than Prince
Edward, more useful than Prince Albert—with an interest in
science and a wordly sense of fashion: two contrary directions in
which design was shifting. Lord Snowdon joined the Council of
Industrial Design.

When, in 1961, Lord Snowdon was installed in a CoID staff
office in the Piccadilly building, helping with the CoID's endeavours to promote 'by all practicable means' design in British
industry, the movement for reform in design was nothing new.
It was over a century since Henry Cole was trying to effect the
alliance of fine art and manufacture, and a hundred years exactly
since William Morris opened his art workshops, and was preaching
to his friends and fellow-craftsmen the importance of simplicity,
sincerity, good materials and sound workmanship. It was, by
then, more than forty years since the Design and Industries
Association was first sounding its tucket and striking its colours.
It was almost thirty years since Frank Pick's Council for Art and
Industry began its conscientious work. It was even (although at
the time it did not seem it), sixteen years since the formation of the
Council of Industrial Design. By this time, the Council employed
204 people; the Board of Trade Grant was £240,000. Government
support for the reformers was substantial. What exactly, at this
stage, could they be said to have achieved?

They had made a certain headway with the manufacturers.
The output of decent tea-cups, well-made tables and neat refrigerators was much higher than it used to be. They had also
made a certain headway with the retailer. The number of shops
stocking decent tea-cups, well-made tables, and Council-approved
products in general was greater. At the same time, the imagination
of the public—and this was most important and extremely interesting—had been seized, much more than ever, by ideas of
good design. Design for modern life: it became a kind of craving.
So much so, as we shall see, that the Council of Industrial Design,
which had encouraged it, was almost left behind.

The thing was that the ideals of the *cognoscenti*, the reverential
feeling for the nicely-designed object, largely through the efforts

of successions of reformers, had gradually reached a much, much wider public.

The cult of special objects for the house, precisely chosen for their individuality and beauty of design, goes back as far as Morris and art furniture workshops and the days when Morris wallpapers adorned most tasteful houses. The singling out of teapots, chairs and tables, books and cushions as positive examples of the designer's art was a Walter Crane obsession: art, he said, should be recognized in the very humblest objects. This intense discrimination, this emphasis upon the designer of the product— *Gimson* chairs, *De Morgan* pottery—essential to the character of the British Arts and Crafts, reached its heights, of course, in Glasgow, with Mackintosh and Walton and Miss Cranston's spotless tea-rooms, in which even the cutlery was specially designed. Wrote Mrs Jessie Newbery, wife of the Director of the Glasgow School of Art, herself a fine embroideress and cushion-cover maker:

'I believe that nothing is common or unclean; that the design and decoration of a pepper pot is as important, in its degree, as the conception of a cathedral.'

This was the principle sophisticated people (the DIA, the *Architectural Review*) hung on to through the century. They glorified the pepper pot. They carried on the cult of the nicely-chosen object; a pleasant household snobbery for people in the know. In the twenties and the thirties, they cultivated craftsmanship: an Edward Barnsley cupboard, a bowl by Bernard Leach. They also came to worship certain new industrial products: a beer mug by Keith Murray, an Edward Bawden tile. At the same time, and increasingly, they loved an *objet trouvé*, or an object which they found to be much better than it seemed: plain old things like porridge bowls were suddenly invested with an awesome sort of glamour. By 1945, pre-dating Terence Conran by almost twenty years, the *Architectural Review* went into raptures over white enamel ironware, red-rimmed and workmanlike; shiny black earthenware jugs (which 'look particularly well if used for milk') and burnt sienna-colour pint mugs 'discovered in a country iron-monger's store'.

By then the war had ended. The aesthetically painful time of taking what you got was shortly to be over. For even if utility furniture and pottery had been a lot more tolerable than anyone had thought, this did not compensate for lack of choice: and in reaction, the urge for great uniqueness was starting up again. This was one good reason for the magic of the Festival, when every designer in the country had his head. This was why the magazines, especially *House and Garden*, could entice their readers out to search for butchers' blocks in hornbeam, antique leeches' urns and other little curios, individual to the point of obscurity. This also explains well the success of the Council of Industrial Design in promoting the idea of special household products designed by special people. The cult of the designer expanded and expanded; by 1962 a discriminating couple would knowledgeably buy a Robin Day convertible, a David Mellor coffee pot, a Brian Asquith boiler, a Martyn Rowlands baby bath, some David Carter castors, a Lucienne Day glasscloth, a chair by Ernest Race, and a Duke's Prize cordless razor designed with utmost elegance by Kenneth Grange. 'Cuttings from *Design*,' wrote a man in Wendover to that magazine, 'are almost our Bible.' In a letter to *The Guardian*, a Wolverhampton reader, wanting advice on the rug to buy, explained:

'I have painted walls and woodwork white and covered the floor with Olive Sullivan's 'Bachelors Button' carpet in burnt orange chestnut. Upholstery is Donald Brothers' unbleached linen mullein cloth. Curtains are orange in a bright Sekers fabric and I am relying upon pictures, books, cushions and rug for bright contrasting accessories. I have found a winner in London Transport's poster 'Greenwich Observatory' which I think looks marvellous against the white walls.'

Such sense and information, such care and such enthusiasm: this was the design-conscious consumer of the sixties.

People knew about designers and design. For there they were in focus everlastingly at Heal's, on every floor, and in an exhibition held in 1960 and entitled 'Designers of the Future'. At the Cotton Board Design and Style Centre in Manchester, under Donald Tomlinson, young textile designers were picked out for publicity: for instance, Pat Albeck, Robert Dodd, Colleen and Gillian Farr with their delicately twining fashionable florals. At Goldsmiths' Hall in London, Graham Hughes the Art Director, was busily promoting the young jewellers and silversmiths: Andrew Grima and John Donald, Gerald Benney, David Mellor, Robert Welch, Keith Tyssen, Keith Redfern, Gerda Flockinger. Commercial firms were boosting their designers: Viners advertised the expertise of Benney, 'famous goldsmith designer'; Old Hall then went one better and described its stainless steel as 'noble metal shaped to perfection by Robert Welch who is recognized as a leading British designer'.

The immense design palaver (which, of course, infuriated basic engineer-designers, whose praises were unsung) happened at a time when youthfulness in general had taken hold of Britain in a rather startling way. The era of the pop group, the boutique and soon the mini-skirt; the heyday of Bazaar and Woolland's 21 Shop; concentration on the personal, the off-beat and the jolly: this sudden burst of fashion made 'design' more popular. Soon what had begun as a small and earnest movement was wilder and much noisier, extremely young and gay. Art nouveau and William Morris were brought back into favour by a larger populace than they had ever known: 'In Carnaby Street,' said the *Daily Express* in 1965, 'Gear have run out of £80 Chesterfields upholstered in William Morris fabrics'; 'William Morris ties the latest vogue', said the *Mail*; 'William Morris wallpapers for bathrooms', said the *Sun*. In *Industrial Design and the Community* Ken Baynes, with inordinate approval, commented on the way that ordinary people and the designer were moving towards one another: 'It is,' he found, 'a *rapprochement* based on a reawakening delight in gaiety, vulgarity, and humour.' To the fury and amazement of some of his profession, Michael Wolff made a statement in the *SIA Journal*: 'Basically it is true that the sort of designers in Britain who have really given people a bang in the past two years are Ken Adams, art director of the James Bond films; Frederick Starke, with his clothes for Cathy Gale; and Ray Cusick, with his Daleks. People like Mary Quant and John Stephen have had the same sort of impact on a more limited age-range. It is their zing, their zest, and their vigorous understanding of what design is all about which should be one of the main contributions of industrial designers to modern society. It'll be a great day when cutlery and furniture designs (to name but two) swing like the Supremes.'

Given the zing and zest, and the concurrent country cottage visions of the glossy magazines; given the great build-up for design and the designer, from William Morris onwards; given the long cult of special household joys, the artistic status symbols, Terence Conran and his Habitat had everything to gain. Habitat, a household shop, 'a shop for switched-on people', opened in South Kensington in 1964. It offered, quite blatantly, 'instant good taste': 'We hope we have taken the foot slogging out of shopping by assembling a wide selection of unusual and top quality goods under our roof. It has taken us a year to complete this pre-digested shopping programme and we are confident that many women will take to this new style of buying with enthusiasm.' Here, on a plate, were all the things the design pundits had hunted for and gloated over all these many years: workmen's mugs and rustic cooking pots and sturdy peasant furniture, baskets, cheap pub glasses, butchers' aprons, wooden toys, an overall good humour and indomitable Britishness. The debt to Arts and Crafts was altogether obvious. But where Arts and Crafts were genuine (or almost), this was phoney: a brilliant and timely commercial pastiche.

'I am not,' wrote Terence Conran, 'interested in "pure" design, which designers sell to other designers, and architects to other architects. I am interested in selling good design to the masses.' The idea of pre-selection—the principle at Heal's and shops like Dunn's of Bromley—was now carried to extremes. Hand-picked by Terence Conran, Habitat was selling a whole fashionable, jovial, pseudo-rural way of life. And all around the country, in small shops called Trend or Scope, Shape or Gear or Spectrum (instead of Svensk and Dansk), pre-selected furnishings and odds and ends were sold with vast conviction and informal, personal service. At Design Design in Lancaster the owners concentrated on things which they themselves had either bought or admired in the past, or things handmade by friends. A firm called Goods & Chattels had a pre-selected stock of storage jars and bentwood, dried dyed flowers and cut-out guardsmen and suchlike for the shopkeepers too ignorant or lazy to pre-select themselves.

In the face of the supermarkets, individual shopkeepers, usually with very little capital, began. None were perhaps braver, more Christian, harder-working than the people who elected to sell proper children's toys: not the mass-produced monstrosities which quickly fell to bits, but strong good toys with play-value, substantial in design. Perhaps they did not know it, but they shared the purist outlook of the parents of John Ruskin, who expected him to play with just a wooden cart and bricks. They certainly acknowledged the influence of Abbatts, who opened shop in Wimpole Street in 1933, stocking stoutest trucks and jigsaws and the bricks which H. G. Wells designed when he wrote *Floor Games*: all toys of lasting worth. By 1967, there were probably a dozen shops with Abbatt's outlook—Galts, John Dobbie, John for Toys, The Owl and the Pussycat, the Boy and Girl Shop, Play and Learn and so on— addicts for sound workmanship, immaculate and bright.

Stressing the importance of design, with fervent feeling for children, life and beauty and the joy of natural wood, individual craftsmen or very small-scale factories produced conscientious toys for these conscientious shops: John Spence's little animals, hand-carved; John Gould's minute, neat, shiny lacquered tugs; Tim Green's honest village bricks; Susan Wynter's whirling roundabouts, and Annette Shelley's cats; Pinny Mice and Tubby Bears from Richmond terrace houses; Sydney Dogs and Lionel Lions and Dilly's Donkeys made in Essex, Pop-Up Rabbits and Black Sambos, Crannie Toys, and Brenda Toys, Coach House Toys, Old Cottage Toys and Ding-Dong hand-made rattles, Simple-Sew Rag Dolls and Make-Your-Own Glove Puppets. Small, wayward cottage industries were fashionably revived.

It was with the instinct that anything is possible Doc Hudson began candle-making, Nigel Quiney started decorating paper-bags and wrapping-paper, Ian Logan put the first of his bold swirling patterns on to plain tin trays. The sense that self-indulgence was now becoming saleable caused Natalie Gibson to embellish tiles with hearts. 'News' in *Design* in 1967 included perspex clocks, paper earrings, patterned pillowcases, and three very jokey cushions that matched up to form a woman. *Design* was less respectful; there was much more shoulder-shrugging. Students left their colleges quite confident and nonchalant. If British manufacturers resisted their ideas, then (like Grierson and like Harcourt) they would sell designs abroad. If British firms showed no enthusiasm for producing whatever they designed, they would market it themselves. This was the attitude that led to little firms like JRM and OMK and Osborne-Little wallpapers, Impetus and Genesis and all the new purveyors of paper chairs and blow-up, knock-down, stack-flat coloured furniture; the dozens of small jewellers; the individual clockmakers.

What is interesting is the way in which a number of these individual enterprises reached a wider market: the way in which Clendenning's experimental furniture was taken up by Race; the way in which the toys designed and made painstakingly by Kristin Baybars and her friends were later mass-produced. What is interesting too is the way designer-craftsmen—designers and/or craftsmen—were so interchangeable. Apart from the few dedicated potters or craft silversmiths, the students leaving college had developed a new attitude: designers were beginning to be far less interested in the means than the results. They cared most for the effect. If industry could make it, and would, then they were happy. If industry would not, then they sat down to it themselves.

All this was quite a change: a rather disconcerting change for the Council of Industrial Design which, through the sixties, had been steaming on respectably, with Centre and with Index, with Awards and Conferences. With Lord Snowdon to the fore (he had given up his job, but worked for the Council as Honorary Adviser) the CoID was still plodding round the industries explaining the virtues of a modern design policy. It had won a famous victory, with questions in the House, over the design of the new Cunard liner, demolishing for ever the tendency in industry to leave design decisions to the Chairman's wife. Its labours had been praised and its achievements had been listed in a House of Lords debate in 1964, in which Viscount Chandos memorably said, 'I never feel comfortable sitting in a chair with the Pytchley hounds in full cry,' and Lord Drumalbyn, Minister of State at the Board of Trade pronounced 'At least we can take comfort from the fact that the task of encouraging design is in good hands', and Baroness Eliot of Harewood said most poignantly, 'I well remember the work of the late Sir Ambrose Heal.'

For that was just the trouble: at this point, the Council seemed much closer to the world of Ambrose Heal than Terence Conran. It looked out of touch with OMK and JRM and swinging London; its zing and zest was minimal; it seemed almost out of date. The dilemma was perceptively explained by Paul Reilly who succeeded Sir Gordon Russell as Director of the CoID, in a leader for the *Architectural Review* in 1967, 'The Challenge of Pop'. Ten years earlier, he said, it had all been so much easier: selectors, armed with yardsticks of Deutscher Werkbund origin, with standards of functional efficiency and fitness for purpose, truth to materials, economy of means, had easily picked out sound design from meretricious; there was then a 'concensus of informed professional opinion in favour of direct, simple, unostentatious, almost neutral solutions'. So much so that the Council, without quite intending it, had seemed to establish its own sober, neutral style.

'London,' wrote Paul Reilly, 'was not yet actually swinging, but she was on the move and rediscovering the excitements of *fin de siecle* colours and patterns. At this point the Design Centre, which until then had spearheaded the campaign against feeble imitations in favour of modern common sense, came into real danger of being hoist with its own petard.' In other words, the Council, so upright and so sensible, was looking rather dowdy, not to say irrelevant. In an SIA Oration, Stephen Spender had cruelly summed up a situation which was to become increasingly obvious through the early 1960s, when the standards of design which the Council propagated were appearing too inflexible, too boring, too austere. He complained of the simple furniture, the unobtrusive yet tasteful hangings, clean-limbed flat irons, innocuous cups and saucers, limpid glass, governessy electric clocks, glacial refrigerators, flat-chested cupboards, disinfected panels of linoleum, all suggesting the young married couple wearing plastic overalls and washing up together after a wholesome and simple meal of foods which are a harmony of oatmeal and pastel shades, at the end of a day in separate offices equipped with electric typewriters. Was this what the DIA ideals had come to? And, if so, what did the Council plan to do?

'Writing in retrospect,' continued Paul Reilly, 'it is easy to give a false impression of deliberate policy decisions being taken by subtle, pliable men sitting round a Council table and recognizing the danger signals and trimming their sails accordingly.' This, he assured readers, was not at all what happened. But one way or another, policy was altered: 'We are shifting, perhaps,' he explained, 'from attachment to permanent universal values to acceptance that a design may be valid at a given time for a given purpose to a given group of people in a given set of circumstances, but that outside those limits it may not be valid at all; and conversely there may be contemporaneous but quite dissimilar solutions that can still be equally defensible for different groups— mini-skirt for the teenager, something less divulging for the matron; painted paper furniture for the young, teak or rosewood for the ageing—and all equally of their times and all equally susceptible to evaluation by a selection committee. All this means is that a product must be good of its kind for the set of circumstances for which it has been designed.'

That attitude was, of course, a very different thing from the other older theories of absolute correctness: the precise, dogmatic principles of Henry Cole; the Arts and Crafts' great love for solid, lasting values; the DIA insistence on interminable worth; Gordon Russell's gentle urge for 'making rich the daily round'. But Paul Reilly was of course a very different kind of person, educated as more of an international modernist than British country craftsman, more cerebral than practical, astute more than romantic, ambitiously benevolent, an opportunist rather than a steady slow advancer, articulate and sociable, quick and diplomatic. His background in the British modern movement of the thirties, with its optimistic principles of taking the broad view, no doubt encouraged Paul Reilly to develop a workable and tolerant philosophy as Director of the Council of Industrial Design: a theory that stretched from paper chairs to great machine tools, from Union Jack dishcloths to, say, cranes or AC motors. From 1960, when he became Director, Paul Reilly seized all possible chances to enlarge.

So it was that the Council of Industrial Design, not content with promoting decent teacups, well-made tables, and neat refrigerators, moved on to bigger things as well: to machine tools and computers, to heavy engineering. It seemed clear that the British engineers' exceptional talent, a century before, for producing a design which was technically and aesthetically admirable, somehow, somewhere, through the years, had gone astray. Since Brunel and Stephenson, Fowler and Baker (with his statement that 'honesty is the guiding light of the designer'), engineers appeared to have lost their sensitivity. It was the old, old story; the Feilden Committee put it bluntly in the report on engineering design submitted in 1963 to the Department of Scientific and Industrial Research, 'British machines are being compared with foreign machines whose designers had understood better the refinements of design and the requirements of the user.'

This was the problem which W. H. Mayall, the new officer for Capital Goods at the Council, had to think about. An inaugural conference in Birmingham convinced him that it was necessary to strengthen the concept of industrial design in engineering and in particular to define its relationship with engineering design. In other words, no one—not design engineers, not industrial designers—knew quite what they were aiming at. Bill Mayall formulated a basic design doctrine, which he carried around like a banner from then on. This doctrine was, briefly, that the design objective contains within it two related aims: the achievement of a functional purpose and the marrying of this purpose to human needs and desires. The former is primarily the engineering design objective, the latter the industrial design objective. Good design is the symbiosis of the two.

This particular movement for reform was the most solemn, the slowest, hardest going and the loneliest of all. Far from the gregarious Arts and Crafts and DIA, remote from the Design Centre Awards and other jollities connected with consumer goods, Bill Mayall, very deadpan, conducted a solitary campaign for design. His strategy was to give lectures and write articles for the engineering press and so awaken interest, then cultivate the people who seemed hopeful and persuade them to take on a professional industrial designer to work with the firm's design engineers. Odd pockets of improvement in different industries affected the converted firm's competitors: for instance, one microscope maker modernized his products and soon the other microscope makers followed suit; a machine-tool manufacturer worked with a designer, and gradually other manufacturers came asking the Record of Designers for a list of possibilities. The five or six companies employing an industrial designer in 1958, through soundly-reasoned argument and sensible persistence, had ten years later multiplied to 200 or more.

As it was in the thirties, it is interesting still, beyond the official propaganda and persuasion, to find in every firm making progress in design, one person pushing hard. Individuals still counted. Rupert Kay at AEI, since 1933, had fought for and achieved, in the end, his own design centre, a fully-equipped model shop, a professional design staff, a series of inter-departmental design conferences: this was, in its day, a considerable victory. J. H. Hilton at Mather & Platt, with consistent encouragement from William Mather, then Director of the General Machinery Division, built up an industrial design unit, establishing a new company design philosophy based on three fundamental notions of SIMPLICITY, STANDARDIZATION and MODERN CONFIGURATION. British design, with emphasis on ergonomics, cybernetics and scientific concepts quite unknown to Henry Cole (though he would soon have learned them), had become a different thing.

Now, more than ever, the industrial designer steered clear of frills and fripperies, avoided the word 'art'. The SIA renamed itself, as hastily as possible, Society of Industrial Artists and Designers, and serious Colleges of Art (and sometimes Craft) were transformed into Colleges of Art and Design. They were businessmen, not artists, Douglas Scott and F. C. Ashford, Alan Kirkbride, Wilkes & Ashmore and avuncular Jack Howe who, insisting that industrial design is a serious activity and designers are sincere and capable individuals, most sanely explained in a *Financial Times* article, the industrial designer's role as a member of a whole industrial team:

'In the field of engineering design there are very few activities which can be performed single-handed, but must of necessity be the result of team work. The design team may be composed of several people, each making his particular contribution in the field in which he is an expert. The industrial designer's contribution is made principally from the point of view of the user, but he must also study the appropriateness of materials and methods of manufacture and combine the results into the final form of the product. All this of course is done in close and constant touch with the other members of the team.

'The engineer's approach is from a different angle because he is concerned primarily with those aspects of design which must be considered in order to meet a given technical specification. He must be concerned with performance, economics, manufacture and cost. The other members of the team also approach the problem from their particular specialist viewpoint and thus it is that we have the same problem approached from different angles but meeting in the middle.

'Teamwork demands a sympathetic human relationship and understanding between every member. The solitary artist or craftsman can go away and work happily on his own without having to worry about other people but in industry this is impossible. A degree of interdependence is called for which can produce jealousies and misunderstandings; prejudice and traditional attitudes must often be broken down before the design process begins to run smoothly. A designer or engineer is involved not only with technicalities but with other people who are also highly trained essential members of the design team—the economist, technician, salesman and manager. Sometimes this involvement can lead to an unsatisfactory tug-of-war of opposing and misunderstood attitudes, or it can add up to a total clearly defined brief and working pattern which is the prerequisite to good design.'

For this was an age of designing by committee: a commercial committee or a government committee, a British Rail or London Transport Design Panel, a committee set up by the Ministry of Public Building and Works to commission design for British embassies, committees convened by the Ministry of Transport to consider new road signs and design new traffic signals. Standard Telephones & Cables appointed Richard Stevens as Industrial Design Manager; Michael Farr set up as management consultant in design; the Royal Society of Arts gave out more medals to encourage 'consistently distinguished design policies'. Industrial design manuals, reports and regulations, directories of house styles, official memoranda on corporate identity, proposals and amendments and paper-work, piled up. And with them the offices of the design consultants, led by Design Research Unit, expanded: as Milner Gray had stated back in 1955 'In my view, a design consultant's services can be best employed through a design committee . . . is it not part of the industrial designer's responsibility to accustom himself to the techniques of inter-departmental administration? I believe it is.'

This was the period of large all-purpose offices, the advent of the general consultant designer: designer of products and packaging and graphics, house styles, exhibitions, offices and shops, space planner and environmental architect, market researcher almost ad infinitum. 'We can,' maintained Hulme Chadwick, 'do almost anything; the scope is unlimited.' Others said the same: Gaby Schreiber, Lewis Woudhuysen, F. H. K. Henrion, Willi de

Majo, Ogle Design, Richard Lonsdale-Hands, Tandy Holford
Mills (employing 45), Allied Industrial Designers (employing 51,
with offices in Brussels, Oslo and Stockholm, with clients in the
Netherlands and Germany and Switzerland, with design teams
operating in French, German, Swedish, English). Eric Marshall,
an American-style cut-and-thrust designer, as far from William
Morris as the British have yet gone, summed up his philosophy:
'The company believes that industrial product design, by defini-
tion, is engineering orientated design and that industrial graphic
design is market orientated. Aesthetics alone are of no value.'

Large-scale designers, through the sixties, had been holding
large-scale conferences on huge and complex subjects, like 'The
Frontiers of Perception'. Professor Misha Black, a monumental
speaker, has addressed the world's designers at ICSID and
UNESCO. Designers have been mingling with psychologists,
ergonomists, statisticians, sociologists and anthropologists, found-
ing Design Research Societies, Ergonomics Research Societies
and so on; holding symposiums on the computer; discussing the
designer in industrialized building; embarking with vast earnestness, and systematic method, on programmes of research which
might well last them for ten years.

The great project of the sixties, which went on year in year out,
was research into design of a hospital bed. This was carried out
by Bruce Archer's Research Unit, attached to the School of
Industrial Design (Engineering) at the Royal College of Art. It
involved a worldwide search of literature: 100,000 documents, a
mammoth filing system. It meant postal enquiries and face-to-face
interviews, evolving a performance specification with 85 statements of user requirements: for instance to accommodate 19
British males out of 20 in comfort a bed must provide a lying
space 86 inches (218 cm) long. The Research Unit built its own
prototypes, identifying 41 critical factors and 85 problem areas.
Every step in the design development was recorded, even the
false trails, and these provided material for subsequent design
methods studies. The Unit submitted the prototype for inspection
and test by selected doctors, nurses and Ministry of Health
technical officers, and built a ward-setting in the RCA workshop
for preliminary assessment. A final year Textile student designed
curtaining and a bedcover to realistic specification; two engineering students designed and built a combined table-locker unit;
another made a unit for lighting, communications and services;
meanwhile the Department of Industrial Glass supplied the ash
tray and non-spill flower vases. A number of simple user tests
were performed in semi-realistic conditions in the ward. Next,
the Ministry of Health undertook to pay for the construction of a
number of beds to this design, and organize and carry out trials
in hospitals, with attendant pathologists, anaesthetists, radiolo-
gists, physiotherapists and work study staff. Next, a team of

nursing tutors and staff nurses examined the prototype in practice, and recorded their comment on standard forms. Next, twenty beds were installed in a 'characteristic hospital' near London for field trials: the ward was observed continuously from 6 in the morning to 10 o'clock at night; every activity involving every bed was recorded on specially devised forms; each patient and each nurse was then subjected to attitude survey interviews by social scientists; there was then a measured study of the energy expended by nurses using old and new bed designs and a methods study on efficiency. The trial was designed to yield information on 60,000 activities, 4,500 samplings and about 270 attitude surveys: in all, about 1,700,000 pieces of information. The forms were designed so that the results could be directly transcribed onto punched tape for computer analysis, answering—or partly answering—the final questions:

1. Does the bed fulfil the specification?
2. Does the specification correctly describe the user's needs?
3. Is the ward-patient-nurse system created by the use of the new specification markedly better or worse than existing systems?

An SIA member wrote to *The Designer* asking if this was not an extremely cumbersome and expensive way of tackling a problem which could be solved as easily by more intuitive methods. And probably it was. But this was not the point: the hospital bed project was building up a body of knowledge, and advancing the status of design. That was the mood, scientific, sociological, infinitely patient, of Bruce Archer and his team, and the other research units, with commercial backing, at Manchester and Hornsey and other intellectual colleges of art. For all this sudden emphasis on systematic method, this insistence on rationalizing design processes, was a bid for intellectual respectability: something which designers before now had done without. In the sixties, the whole set-up for the training of designers had become much more ambitious, broader-based, more literate. The Diploma in Art and Design, an equivalent of a university degree, was introduced in 40 colleges in England and Wales. Five of them also offered post-diploma studies. Half of these big colleges by now had been absorbed into centrally-administered, large polytechnic schemes. Besides, with trumpets blowing and specially-embroidered ceremonial robes, the Royal College of Art had now been granted university status, and gave master's degrees to its students of design.

With the news that the Council of Industrial Design was likely very soon to be incorporated in a National Design Council, a larger, richer, and more influential body, covering the whole range of industry, from light to heavy and from craft-based to highly-technical, a new phase for reform of design appeared to be beginning. An age of anonymity for the designer. An age of teamwork and systematic method and industrial design manuals.

A time for talk of total-activity-patterns and the designer's contribution to the expanding technological universe.

How William Morris and Voysey would have hated it. How hard Harry Peach would have tried to understand it. But how very satisfactory, neat, tidy and rewarding, Henry Cole would have found it, after all.

POSTSCRIPT

1971, and one has a distinct feeling that design—or anyway 'design'—has had its heyday. The glorious visions of a nicely designed Britain now seems a little faded. The old reformers have died, or been subdued.

It has suddenly become extremely obvious to designers that the notion of a close, harmonious, idealistic collaboration between designer, manufacturer and shopkeeper—the theory so dear to the hearts of the reformers, from the Council of Industrial Design and D.I.A. right back as far as Cole and his forays into industry—is just a bit too hopeful. One finds these days, when talking to designers leaving college, that this is not the thing they really aim for any more.

The future, as far as one can see it at the moment, seems to be less with official propaganda and high-minded little groups of design enthusiasts, more with designers themselves getting out and doing things. Young designers seem less inclined to work within a ready-made system of industrial consultancy. They more often want to make their individual contribution, and within the next few years the numbers of designer-manufacturers, designer-distributors and designer-shopkeepers is bound to multiply.

Hopes for all things bright and beautiful have dwindled. But other ideas and attitudes have overtaken them and, realistically, the future of design in Britain now lies with the British designers themselves.

Standard Bank

240

241

242

240
Stefan Buzas and Alan Irvine
Entrance to Standard Bank,
Northumberland Avenue, London,
1966.

241
Stefan Buzas and Alan Irvine
Interior, Standard Bank, 1966.

242
Clive Bacon
Linking/stacking chairs in beech
made by Design Furnishing
Contracts, 1963.

243
Ronald Carter
'Brompton' chair made by Dancer
and Hearne, 1963.

243

244
Robin Day
Polypropylene stacking chair made
by Hille, 1961.

245
Conran Design Group
Kitchen furniture, 1966.

246
Ernest Race
'Sheppey' easy chair and settees
made by Race, 1961–2.

247
Nigel Walters
'International' kitchen units made by
F. Wrighton, 1968.

244

245

246

247

248
Robert Heritage
'Queen Elizabeth II' restaurant
chairs made by Race, 1967.

249
Martin Grierson and Keith Townend
Pre-formed plywood units made by
Kandya, installed in laboratory at
Imperial College, London, 1961.

250
Nicholas Frewing
'Flexible' chair made by Race, 1966.

251
Ronald Carter
Storage units for Consort, 1965.

248

249

250

252

254

252
OMK Design
Chair in chrome-plated tubular
steel and leather, 1966.

253
Polycell Design Group
Nursery furniture in corrugated
fibreboard, 1967.

254 and 255
R. V. Exton and P. K. Wigglesworth
Tubular steel dining table and chairs
made by Plush Kicker, 1968.

255

256

256
Zeev Aram and Associates
Floor-standing ashtray for
Simpson's, London, 1967.

257
Zeev Aram and Associates
Executive desks system, 1965.

258
Zeev Aram and Associates
Floor mirror for Simpson's, 1967.

259 and 260
Zeev Aram and Associates
Interior, Trend Department,
Simpson's, 1967.

258

259

261

262

263

261
Frederick Scott
Seating in polyurethane foam made by Hille, 1968.

262
Max Clendenning
Dining furniture in pre-formed plywood made by Race, 1966–7.

263
Robin Day
'Disque' knock-down table made by Hille, 1967.

264
Peter Murdoch
'Hexagon' seating in polyurethane foam made by Hille, 1968.

264

265

266

267

265
Howard Carter
'Sunflower' printed cotton made by
Heal Fabrics, 1962.

266
Gillian Farr
'Ambergate' satin union fabric made
by Bernard Wardle, 1964.

267
Shirley Craven
Printed cotton satin made by Hull
Traders, 1963.

268

268
Shirley Craven
'Five' printed linen and cotton made
by Hull Traders, 1966.

269
Haydon Williams
'Extension' printed cotton made by
Heal Fabrics, 1967.

269

270

271

272

270
Cathryn Netherwood
'Concentric' satin cotton made by
Heal Fabrics, 1968.

271
Tamesa Fabrics
'Allegro' two-tone weave for
upholstery, 1963.

272
Tamesa Fabrics
'Visor' striped textured cotton, 1967.

273
William Robertson and Peter Simpson
'Glendale' woven linen/rayon/cotton
made by Donald Brothers, 1963.

273

274

275

276

274
Lucienne Day
'Signum' carpet made by
I. & C. Steele, 1965.

275
Lucienne Day
'Big Circle' carpet made by
I. & C. Steele, 1965.

276
Mary Yonge
'Magnetic' carpet made by
I. & C. Steele, 1965.

277

277
Catherine Beevers
'Katrina' carpet made by Andrew
Gaskell, 1965.

278
Catherine Beevers
'Scene Collection' wallpaper made
by Crown, 1967.

278

279

280

281

282

283

279
Robert Welch
Cast-iron table heater and casseroles, 1965.

280
Tarquin Cole and John Minshaw of Ceramic Consultants
Stoneware casseroles made by Govancroft, 1964.

281
Frank Thrower
'Victoria' wine suite made by Dartington Glass, 1964.

282
David Queensberry and Jessie Tait
Tableware made by Midwinter, 1965.

283
Robert Welch
Cast-iron candlesticks, 1962.

284
David Mellor
'Embassy' silver teapot designed and made for Ministry of Public Building and Works, 1962.

285
Robert Welch
'Alveston' stainless steel teapot made by Old Hall, 1963.

286
David Mellor
Polystyrene cutlery made by Cross Paperware, 1970.

287
Robert Welch
Condiment set in stainless steel and plastic made by Old Hall, 1963.

288
David Mellor
Tea and coffee pots in stainless steel and plastic made by J. R. Bramah, 1969.

284

286

287

288

289

290

291

292

289
Robert Welch
'Merlin' electric alarm clock made by
Westclox, 1962.

290
D. M. R. Brunton
'Corinthian' electric fire made by
Belling, 1963.

291
Kenneth Grange
'Vecta' Brownie camera made by
Kodak, 1962.

292
Kenneth Grange
'Courier' electric shaver made by
Milward, 1961.

293
Robert Heritage
'Quartet Major' light fittings made
by Rotaflex, 1964.

294
Norman Stevenson
Bells and bell pushes made by
Friedland, 1963.

295
Kenneth Grange
'Classic' electric iron made by
Morphy-Richards, 1966.

296
Hulme Chadwick
Garden shears made by Wilkinson
Sword, 1963.

297
Joy and Malcolm Wilcox
Cut-out doll sheet made by Sari
Fabrics, 1964.

298
Martyn Rowlands
Telephone made by Standard
Telephones and Cables, 1963–4.

299
John Gould
Toy train made by Nicoltoys, 1962.

295

296

297

298

299

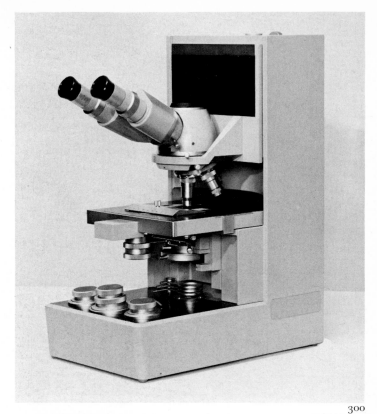

300
Noel London and Howard Upjohn
'Patholux' microscope for Vickers
Instruments, 1964.

301
Noel London and Howard Upjohn
'1901' system for '1900' computer
series, made by International
Computers, 1965.

300

301

302

302
R. David Carter
Gas fitting from Gas-Flo system
developed by Wales Gas Board, 1967.

303
David Mellor
Gear-measuring machine for
J. Goulder, 1965.

304

305

307

304
Royal College of Art, School of Industrial Design (Engineering) Research Unit (Director, Dr L. Bruce Archer)
Prototype hospital bed, developed 1963–7.

305
Mather and Platt Industrial Design Department with Electrical Engineering Designers
Flameproof motors, 1966.

306
David Mellor
Traffic signal system designed with Ministry of Transport, 1969.

307
Jock Kinneir
Directional traffic sign system designed for Highway Authorities, 1963.

306

308

309

310

308
Alex Moulton
Moulton Major bicycle, 1963.

309
Alec Issigonis
Mini Minor made by British Motor
Corporation, 1959. De luxe version,
1967.

310
Douglas Scott Associates
Hy-Mac 580B Excavator made by
Rhymney Engineering, 1964.

311
*Misha Black and James Williams of
Design Research Unit*
Beagle B206 made by Beagle
Aircraft, 1961.

312
*Misha Black and J. Beresford-Evans of
Design Research Unit*
25 kv. 3,200 h.p. AC/electric
locomotive designed for British
Railways, 1956.

Chronological Table

1836   Mr Ewart's Select Committee reported to the Government on 'the best means of extending a knowledge of the arts and the principles of design among the people (especially the manufacturing population) of the country'.

1837   Normal School of Design established at Somerset House (later to develop into Royal College of Art).

1841   *True Principles of Pointed or Christian Architecture* by Augustus Welby Northmore Pugin published.

1844   Society for the Encouragement of Arts, Manufactures and Commerce held first Exhibition of the Products of National Industry.

1846   Felix Summerly (alias Henry Cole) won silver medal for design for tea-set in Society of Arts Competition.
Society of Arts began to give annual prizes to students of design in art schools.

1847   Summerly's Art Manufactures founded.
Society of Arts granted Royal Charter.

1849   *Journal of Design and Manufactures* first published.
Seven Lamps of Architecture by John Ruskin published.

1851   Great Exhibition held in Hyde Park.

1851–3   *Stones of Venice* by John Ruskin published.

1852   Ornamental Art Collection opened at Marlborough House (later to form basis for Victoria and Albert Museum).

1856   Department of Practical Art created (later to become Department of Science and Art) at South Kensington under Henry Cole.
Grammar of Ornament by Owen Jones published.

1857   *Report on the Present State of Design as Applied to Manufactures* by Richard Redgrave published.

1861   Morris, Marshall and Faulkner, Fine Art Workmen, issued first prospectus.

1862	International Exhibition held in South Kensington.
1868	*Hints on Household Taste* by Charles Eastlake published.
1875	Arthur Lasenby Liberty opened shop in Regent Street, specializing in Oriental merchandise.
1877	Society for Protecting Ancient Buildings (Anti-Scrape) formed.
1880	Art Furniture Alliance opened by Christopher Dresser in Bond Street.
1881	George Edmund Street died.
1882	Century Guild formed by Arthur H. Mackmurdo.
	Sir Henry Cole died.
1884	Art Workers' Guild founded.
	Home Art and Industries Association formed.
1888	Arts and Crafts Exhibition Society founded, holding successful exhibitions in 1888, 1889, 1890, 1893 and 1896.
	National Association for Advancement of Art and its Application to Industry founded.
	C. R. Ashbee formed Guild and School of Handicraft.
1890	Kenton & Co., furniture workshops, opened by Lethaby, Gimson and Sidney Barnsley.
	William Morris founded Kelmscott Press.
1893	*The Studio* first published.
1895	Bing's shop, L'Art Nouveau, opened in Paris, selling a large number of Arts and Crafts from England.
1896	Society of Designers established 'To advance the arts of design and the status of designers; and for friendly intercourse' (but little appears to have been heard of it again).
	Central School opened 'to encourage the industrial application of decorative art' and Lethaby appointed joint Principal.
	Hermann Muthesius attached to German Embassy in London for research into British architecture and crafts.
	William Morris died.
1897–99	Glasgow School of Art, first phase, built to design by Charles Rennie Mackintosh.
1898	Heal's first catalogue of Plain Oak Furniture produced.
	Northern Art Workers' Guild held first exhibition.
	Walter Crane appointed Principal of the Royal College of Art but resigned the same year.
1899	Grand Duke of Hesse's artistic colony at Darmstadt established with designs for the Palace by Baillie Scott and Mackintosh.
1900	Paris Exhibition: British designers represented (Heal's winning two silver medals).
	Ernest Gimson and the Barnsley brothers settled in the Cotswolds.
	Lethaby became first Professor at the Royal College of Art (retiring as Principal of the Central School in 1911).
1901	Glasgow International Exhibition.
	Die Englische Baukunst der Gegenwart by Hermann Muthesius published in Germany.
1902	Turin International Exhibition.

Ashbee's Guild of Handicraft moved to Chipping Campden, Gloucestershire.

1904   Christopher Dresser died.

1904–5   *Das Englische Haus*, 3 illustrated volumes by Hermann Muthesius, published in Germany.

1905   Exhibition of Cheap Cottages at Letchworth, sponsored by *The Spectator*.

1910   Lewis Day died.

1911   Report of the Departmental Committee on the Royal College of Art recommended closure of the College.

1914   Harold Stabler, Ambrose Heal, Harry Peach and others visited the Werkbund Exhibition in Cologne and returned convinced of the importance of designing for machine production.

1915   Government-sponsored wartime exhibition of German industrial design held at Goldsmiths Hall.
Design and Industries Association founded with 199 members.
DIA held first exhibition 'Design and Workmanship in Printing' at Whitechapel Gallery.
Walter Crane died.

1916   DIA exhibited at Arts and Crafts Exhibition at Burlington House.

1918   Cecil Brewer died.

1919   *Art and Industry* pamphlet issued by Ministry of Reconstruction.

1920   British Institute of Industrial Art founded and gallery opened in Knightsbridge but official grant withdrawn the next year.
Federation of British Industry formed Industrial Art Committee, with Charles Tennyson as Chairman, 'to consider the question of industrial art in this country'.
DIA 'Exhibition of Household Things' held at Whitechapel Gallery.
Ernest Gimson died.

1923   Exhibition of 'Industrial Art Today'.
Francis Meynell founded Nonesuch Press.

1924   Designers' Register and Employment Bureau opened by Industrial Art Committee of FBI.
Royal Society of Arts, encouraged by Sir Frank Warner, began series of annual competitions for design open to all British subjects.
W. A. S. Benson died.

1925   Paris Exhibition.
Sidney Barnsley died.

1927   DIA exhibited at Leipzig Fair.

1928   Chermayeff exhibition held at Waring & Gillow.
Gordon Russell exhibited furniture at Powell's London showroom.
Charles Rennie Mackintosh died.

1929   'Industrial Art for the Slender Purse', British Institute of Industrial Art exhibition, held at Victoria and Albert Museum.

Gordon Russell opened shop in Wigmore Street.

Jack Pritchard commissioned stand from Le Corbusier for Venesta at Building Trades Exhibition.

The Face of the Land, DIA Year Book, published.

1930   Society of Industrial Artists founded.

Memorandum on State-aided Art Education published by Industrial Art Committee of FBI, recommending that regional colleges should be established and the Royal College of Art reorganized.

Report on Handicrafts in Elementary Schools published by LCC.

Report on Design in the Cotton Industry published by H.M. Inspectors.

1931   Board of Trade appointed Committee on Art and Industry, under Lord Gorell.

Exhibition of Swedish Art held in London.

William Richard Lethaby died.

1932   Association of Artists in Commerce founded (but never came to much).

Raymond McGrath, Wells Coates and Serge Chermayeff designed interiors for new BBC building.

Report on Art and Education, in particular industrial art exhibitions, published by Gorell committee.

1933   Dorland Hall exhibition held, in collaboration with DIA.

DIA exhibitions of model houses held in Manchester and Welwyn.

BBC held series of talks, 'Design in Modern Life'.

Paul and Marjorie Abbatt opened toyshop in Wimpole Street.

Ghastly Good Taste, by John Betjeman, published.

1934   Council for Art and Industry set up by Board of Trade, with Frank Pick as Chairman, to encourage good design, 'especially in relation to manufacturers'.

Pick Council held small exhibition of Silverware at Victoria and Albert Museum.

Second, less successful, Dorland Hall exhibition held.

DIA exhibition held in Birmingham.

'Exhibition of Modern Living' held at Whiteley's.

Walter Gropius arrived in England, and left again two years later.

Art and Industry by Herbert Read published.

Memorandum on Art Education, with particular reference to the Royal College of Art, sent by the DIA to the Board of Education.

1935   'British Art in Industry' exhibition held at Burlington House.

Pick Council held pottery exhibition at Victoria and Albert Museum.

Orion, architect Brian O'Rorke, launched by Orient Line.

Industrial Design Partnership founded by Milner Gray, Misha Black and others.

Report on Industrial Art submitted by Nugent Committee to Minister of Education.

Memorandum on industrial art training for management and staff of firms (full-time and part-time) and for foremen, travellers and salesmen, published by Industrial Art Committee of FBI.

Report on Education for the Consumer, particularly training in design in elementary and secondary schools, published by Pick Council.

Harold Stabler died.

1936 First 10 Designers for Industry appointed by Royal Society of Arts (from 1937, *Royal* Designers for Industry): Douglas Cockerell, Eric Gill, James Hogan, J. H. Mason, H. G. Murphy, Keith Murray, Tom Purvis, George Sheringham, Harold Stabler, Fred Taylor, C. F. A. Voysey.

National Register of Industrial Art Designers formed by Board of Trade on recommendation of Pick Council.

Committee on Advanced Education in London, under Viscount Hambledon, appointed by Board of Education.

Pick Council held exhibition of domestic metalwork.

'Exhibition of Everyday Things' at Royal Institute of British Architects.

'Seven Architects' Exhibition at Heal's.

Dunbar Hay furnishing shop opened in Albemarle Street.

Crofton Gane commissioned pavilion for Royal Show, Bristol, from Marcel Breuer and F. R. S. Yorke.

Report on The Working-Class Home: its Furnishing and Equipment by Mrs C. G. Tomrley, published by Pick Council.

Harry Peach died.

1937 Paris Exhibition included British Pavilion by Pick Council.

Working-Class Home exhibition, based on Pick Council report, held at Building Centre.

BBC Talks on Design by Anthony Bertram held with concurrent travelling exhibitions by DIA.

Industrial Art in England by Nickolaus Pevsner published.

Report on Design and the Designer in Industry published by Pick Council.

Report on Advanced Art Education in London, published by Hambledon Committee recommending that 'a new orientation should be given to the Royal College'.

Proposal for an Industrial Art Centre completed by Pick Council but never published.

1938 Glasgow Exhibition.

Royal Designers for Industry appointed: Reco Capey, E. Gordon Craig, Milner Gray, Percy Metcalfe, Ethel Mairet.

Royal Society of Arts Industrial Bursaries Competition began.

Good Furnishing Group formed by Geoffrey Dunn, Crofton Gane, Gordon Russell and others.

1939 Central Institute of Art and Design formed, to safeguard artists' and designers' interests in wartime.

Royal Designers for Industry appointed: Laurence Irving, Sir

Ambrose Heal, Brian O'Rorke.

1940   Cotton Board Fashion Design & Style Centre opened in Manchester.
Royal Designers for Industry appointed: Susie Cooper, E. W. Grieve, A. B. Read, Gordon Russell, Percy Delf Smith, Allan Walton, Anna Zinkeisen.

1941   Royal Designer for Industry appointed: Duncan Grant.
C. F. A. Voysey died.
Frank Pick died.

1942   Utility Furniture Committee and subsequently Design Panel, Chairman Gordon Russell, set up by Board of Trade.
DIA, with Army Bureau of Current Affairs, began to send mobile design exhibitions round army camps, art galleries and schools.
Arthur H. Mackmurdo died.
C. R. Ashbee died.

1943   Report on 'Industrial Design and Art in Industry' completed, but not published, by sub-committee under Cecil Weir (set up by Post-War Export Trade Committee of Department of Overseas Trade), recommending the establishment of a Central Design Council.
Design Research Unit set up by Marcus Brumwell, Misha Black, Milner Gray and others, with Herbert Read as first manager.
Royal Designers for Industry appointed: Charles Holden, Barnes Wallis.

1944   Report on Art Training by Meynell-Hoskin Committee, submitted to Board of Trade and Education, supported the idea of a Central Design Council, recommending that it should be a grant-aided body.
Proposals for a Central Design Council and Industrial Design Centre published by Industrial Art Committee of FBI.
Council of Industrial Design (with separate Scottish Committee) formed 'to promote by all practicable means the improvement of design in the products of British industry': first Chairman was Sir Thomas Barlow; first Director, S. C. Leslie.
Rayon Industry Design Centre established.
The Missing Technician in Industrial Production by John Gloag published.
Royal Designers for Industry appointed: Wells Coates, Sir Geoffrey de Havilland, Enid Marx, Charles Nicholson, R. D. Russell.

1945   'Design for the Home' exhibition, designed by Milner Gray, held by Council for the Encouragement of Music and the Arts.
'Historical and British Wallpapers' exhibition, designed by Eric Brown and Stefan Buzas, held at National Gallery.
CoID Record of Designers developed from National Register of Industrial Art Designers.
Primavera opened by Henry Rothschild in Sloane Street.
Royal Designer for Industry appointed: Francis Meynell.

1946   'Britain Can Make It' exhibition held by CoID at Victoria and Albert Museum, designer James Gardner.

Design and Research Centre for the Gold, Silver and Jewellery Industries established.

National Diploma in Design introduced in art schools, with emphasis on specialization.

Report on the Training of the Industrial Designer completed by CoID but never published.

Report *The Visual Arts* sponsored by Dartington Hall trustees, published in collaboration with PEP.

1947   Gordon Russell succeeded S. C. Leslie as Director of the Council of Industrial Design; Dr Ralph Edwards succeeded Sir Thomas Barlow as Chairman.

'Enterprise Scotland' exhibition held by CoID in Edinburgh.

Royal Designers for Industry appointed: James Gardner, Robert Goodden, Ashley Havinden.

1948   Robin Darwin appointed Principal of Royal College of Art.

'Design at Work' exhibition of products by Royal Designers for Industry sponsored by RSA and CoID.

Robin Day and Clive Latimer won prize in International Low-cost Furniture Competition, Museum of Modern Art, New York.

Central Institute for Art and Design disbanded.

Royal Designer for Industry appointed: Christian Barman.

1949   CoID exhibited abroad for first time, in 'International Exhibition of Industrial Design' in Amsterdam.

BBC series of programmes, 'Looking At Things', for school-children began.

Royal Designers for Industry appointed: Edward Bawden, Barnett Freedman, Roger Furse, Eric Ottaway.

1950   Royal Designers for Industry appointed: Edward Molyneux, Sir James McNeill, Alastair Morton.

1951   Festival of Britain: South Bank Exhibition Design Group, Hugh Casson, James Holland, James Gardner, Ralph Tubbs, Misha Black.

'Living Traditions of Scotland' exhibition held in Edinburgh.

Exhibition of Industrial Power held in Glasgow.

Des.RCA first given to students awarded design diplomas at Royal College of Art.

Royal Designers for Industry appointed: Hugh Casson, J. Laurent Giles.

1952   Exhibition of Victorian and Edwardian Decorative Arts at Victoria and Albert Museum.

CoID Street Furniture design competition.

Time-Life building in Bond Street completed, with interiors co-ordinated by Hugh Casson and Misha Black.

1953   Walter J. Worboys succeeded Dr Ralph Edwards as Chairman of the CoID.

'Register Your Choice' DIA exhibition, at Charing Cross.
Royal Designers for Industry appointed: John Waterer, Ernest Race.

1954   Government approved establishment of The Design Centre for British Industries.

First Royal Society of Arts Bicentenary Medal, for people who 'in a manner other than as industrial designers have exerted an exceptional influence in promoting art and design in British industry', awarded to Sir Colin Anderson.

Royal Designer for Industry appointed: William Lyons.

1955   *Design in British Industry* by Michael Farr published.

Royal Designer for Industry appointed: Uffa Fox.

RSA Bicentenary Medal awarded to Sir Charles Tennyson.

1956   Design Centre, Haymarket, opened by Duke of Edinburgh.

'Management of Design' conference organized by CoID.

British Railways Design Panel set up; George Williams Director of Design.

Royal Designer for Industry appointed: Reynolds Stone.

RSA Bicentenary Medal awarded to Sir Walter Worboys.

SIA Design Medal awarded to Milner Gray.

Gordon Russell knighted.

Design magazine began to include regular reviews of engineering products.

1957   Scottish Design Centre opened by Scottish Committee of CoID.

'Make or Mar', DIA exhibition, held at Charing Cross.

Report on Art Examinations submitted to Minister of Education by Freeman Committee on Art Examinations, recommending greater administrative freedom for individual colleges.

Royal Designer for Industry appointed: Misha Black.

RSA Bicentenary Medal awarded to Sir Ernest Goodale.

SIA Design Medal awarded to Jan van Krimpen.

First Design Centre Awards selected by Milner Gray, Professor R. Y. Goodden, Brian O'Rorke, Professor R. D. Russell, Astrid Sampe:

Pyrex ovenware—designers, John D. Cochrane in conjunction with Milner Gray and Kenneth Lamble of Design Research Unit; maker, James A. Jobling.

Convertible bed settee—designer, Robin Day; maker, Hille.

Rotaflex lampshade—designers, John and Sylvia Reid; maker, Rotaflex.

Rayburn convector fire—designer, David Ogle; maker, Allied Ironfounders.

Television set—designer, Robin Day; maker, Pye.

Midwinter Melmex plastics ware—designers, A. H. Woodfull and John Vale; maker, Streetly, for W. R. Midwinter.

Impasto wallpaper—designer, Audrey Levy; maker, The Wall Paper Manufacturers.

Strawberry Hill tableware—designers, Victor Skellern and

Millicent Taplin; maker, Wedgwood.

Pride cutlery and flatware—designer, David Mellor; maker, Walker & Hall.

Connoisseur wine glasses—designer, S. Fogelberg; maker, Thomas Webb.

Flamingo furnishing cotton—designer, Tibor Reich; maker, Tibor.

Imperial Axminster carpet—designer, Lucienne Day; maker, Tomkinsons.

1958 'The Design Centre Comes to Newcastle' exhibition: first in series of promotions in provincial stores.

'Industrial Design and the Engineering Industries' conference organized by the CoID in Birmingham.

Wells Coates died.

RSA Bicentenary Medal awarded to John Gloag.

SIA Design Medal awarded to Robin Day.

Design Centre Awards selected by Sir Walter Worboys, Noel Carrington, Geoffrey Dunn, Wyndham Goodden, Jack Howe:

Carlton lavatory basin—designers, staff; maker, Shanks.

Satina pendant lighting fitting—designer, Nigel Chapman; maker, Hailwood and Ackroyd Ltd for AEI.

Hiflo bibcock tap—designers, staff; maker, Barking Brassware.

Knifecut pruner—designers, staff with Hulme Chadwick; maker, Wilkinson Sword.

Occasional chair—designer, J. N. Stafford; maker, Stafford Furniture.

Tallent paraffin oil convector heater—designers, staff; maker, Tallent Engineering.

Prestwick range of suitcases—designer, K. H. Paterson; maker, S. E. Norris.

Phantom Rose handscreen printed wallpaper—designer, Audrey Levy; maker, The Wall Paper Manufacturers.

Old Hall stainless steel toast rack—designer, Robert Welch; maker, Old Hall.

Conference tableware—designers, Tom Arnold (shape), Pat Albeck (pattern); maker, Ridgway.

Hamilton sideboard—designer, Robert Heritage; maker, Archie Shine.

Adam woven textile—designer, Keith Vaughan; maker, Edinburgh Weavers.

Vision Net lace curtaining—designer, F. G. Hobden and staff; maker, Clyde Manufacturing.

Royal Gobelin Axminster body carpet—designers, Neville and Mary Ward; maker, Tomkinsons.

Queensberry enamelled cast iron ovenware—designer, David Queensberry; maker, Enamelled Iron & Steel Products.

Artkurl Wilton broadloom carpets—designers, staff; maker, William C. Gray.

Riviera tablecloths and napkins—designer, Arthur Ingham; maker, James Finlay.

Gold Seal baby bath—designer, Martyn O. Rowlands; maker, Ekco Plastics.

Minster printed textile—designer, Humphrey Spender; maker, Edinburgh Weavers.

Vistavu slide viewer—designers, Harold R. Stapleton assisted by Howard Upjohn; maker, Rank Precision Industries.

1959   National Advisory Council on Art Education, under Sir William Coldstream, formed.

CoID awarded Gran Premio Internazionale la Rinascente Compasso d'Oro in Milan.

Design Centre labelling scheme began.

Oriana launched by Orient Line.

Sir Gordon Russell retired as Director of CoID.

Sir Ambrose Heal died.

Royal Designers for Industry appointed: Robin Day, Abram Games, F. H. K. Henrion, Hans Schleger, Berthold Wolpe.

RSA Bicentenary Medal awarded to Frank Mercer.

SIA Design Medal awarded to Tapio Wirkkala.

Duke of Edinburgh's first Prize for Elegant Design awarded by Lady Casson, Sir Basil Spence, John Summerson and Audrey Withers to C. W. F. Longman, designer (in association with Edward G. Wilkes) of Packaway refrigerator made by Prestcold Division of Pressed Steel Company.

Design Centre Awards selected by Sir Colin Anderson, Geoffrey Dunn, F. H. K. Henrion, Jack Howe and Monica Pidgeon:

Swoe garden tool—designers, staff, with Hulme Chadwick; maker, Wilkinson Sword.

Ilford K1 professional tripod—designer, Walter Kennedy; maker, Ilford.

Ellipse series lighting fittings—designer, Paul Boissevain; maker, The Merchant Adventurers.

Pride EPNS teaset—designer, David Mellor; maker, Walker & Hall.

Aristocrat socket chisels—designer, staff; maker, Ward & Payne.

Planit system: ceramic glazed tiles—designer, Derek Hodgkinson; maker, H. & R. Johnson.

Flamingo easy chair—designer, Ernest Race; maker, Race Furniture.

Fluorescent kitchen light—designers, John and Sylvia Reid; maker, Atlas.

Lever handle—designer, Roger Peach; maker, Dryad Metal.

Mandala Wilton body carpet—designer, Audrey Tanner; maker, Carpet Manufacturing.

Queen-heater solid fuel room heater—designer, David Mellor; maker, Grahamston Iron Co.

Malindi printed furnishing fabric—designer, Gwenfred Jarvis; maker, Liberty.

Piazza plastics coated fabric—designer, Edward Pond; maker, Bernard Wardle.

Inglewood woven furnishing fabric—designer, Humphrey Spender, maker, Edinburgh Weavers.

Circular dining table—designer, Hassan El-Hayani; maker, Design Furniture for the New Furniture Design Group.

1960   Paul Reilly succeeded Sir Gordon Russell as Director of CoID; Sir Duncan Oppenheim succeeded Sir Walter Worboys as Chairman.

'Designers of the Future' exhibition held at Heal's.

Competition for better litter bins sponsored by CoID.

First Report on Art Education by Coldstream Committee submitted to Minister of Education, recommending new courses of a higher standard to replace the National Diploma in Design.

Industrial Design (Engineering) Research Unit set up at Royal College of Art, under Bruce Archer.

Royal Designers for Industry appointed: Stanley Morison, Basil Spence.

RSA Bicentenary medal awarded to J. Cleveland Belle.

Duke's Price for Elegant Design awarded by Lady Casson, Robin Darwin, Gaby Schreiber and Basil Spence to Neal French and David White for Spode Apollo tableware made by W. T. Copeland.

Design Centre Awards selected by Professor Misha Black, J. Beresford-Evans, F. H. K. Henrion and Jo Pattrick:

Street lighting columns and lanterns—designer, Richard Stevens; maker, Abacus.

Irish linen glass towels—designer, Lucienne Day; maker, Thomas Somerset.

Chelsea lighting fittings—designers, Richard Stevens and P. Rodd; maker, Atlas Lighting.

Le Bosquet printed cotton satin—designer, Shirley Craven; maker, Hull Traders.

Brownie camera—designers, staff with Kenneth Grange; maker, Kodak.

Low voltage display fitting—designer, Richard Stevens; maker, Atlas Lighting.

Queensberry Ware nursery china—designers, David Queensberry (shape), Bernard Blatch (pattern); maker, Crown Staffordshire.

Pannus wallpaper—designer, Humphrey Spender; maker, The Wall Paper Manufacturers.

Lemington glass vases—designer, R. Stennett-Willson; maker, Osram.

Fiesta melamine plates—designer, Ronald E. Brookes; maker, Brookes and Adams.

Vynide coated fabric—designers, staff; maker, ICI.

Formation Furniture office desk units—designers, Yorke, Rosenberg and Mardall; maker, Bath Cabinet Makers.

Ely Stripe woven furnishing—designers, staff; maker, Donald Brothers.

Anniversary Ware oval casseroles—designers, John and Sylvia Reid; maker, Izons.

Judge stainless steel stewpans—designers, Misha Black and Ronald Armstrong of DRU; maker, Ernest Stevens.

Denison Vision Net drip-dry furnishing lace—designer, F. G. Hobden; maker, Clyde.

Royal Gobelin Axminster carpet—designer, Graham Tutton; maker, Tomkinsons.

1961   National Council for Diplomas in Art and Design, under Sir John Summerson, set up on Coldstream Council's recommendation as an independent self-governing body to administer the award of diplomas.

Antony Armstrong-Jones (later the Earl of Snowdon) joined staff of CoID.

'Design Policy for Corporate Buying', international design congress organized in London by CoID.

Modern Jewellery Exhibition held at Goldsmiths' Hall.

CoID Street Furniture exhibition installed on South Bank.

Royal Designers for Industry appointed: Stefan Buzas, Jack Howe.

RSA Bicentenary medal awarded to Audrey Withers.

SIA Design Medal awarded to Abram Gaines.

Duke's Prize for Elegant Design awarded by Sir Kenneth Clark, Robin Darwin, Jane Drew and Gaby Schreiber to Eric Marshall for Rio transistor radio made by Ultra.

Design Centre Awards selected by Whitney W. Straight, Neville Condor, Jo Pattrick, J. M. Richards, and Gary Schreiber:

Kodaslide 40 slide projector—designers, staff with Kenneth Grange; maker, Kodak.

Cormorant folding outdoor chair—designer, Ernest Race; maker, Race Furniture.

Table mirror—designer, Colin Beales; maker, Peter Cuddon.

Towel rail—designer and maker, Peter Cuddon.

Town Number One litter bin—designers, Derek Goad and John Ricks; maker, G. A. Harvey.

Adjustable spotlights—designers, John and Sylvia Reid; maker, Rotaflex.

Monte Carlo carving set—designer, G. G. Bellamy; maker, George Wostenholm.

Chef Royal saucepans—designers, Berkeley Associates; maker, Curran.

Orbit furniture castors—designers, staff with R. David Carter; maker, Joseph Gillott.

266

> Redfyre Centramatic 35 oil fired boiler—designers, staff with Brian Asquith; maker, Redfyre.
>
> Form unit furniture—designer, Robin Day; maker, Hille.
>
> Paragon chemical closet—designer, Martyn Rowlands; maker, Racasan.

1962 First conference on systematic design methods held at Imperial College, London.

Second report of Coldstream Council, on vocational courses in Colleges and Schools of Art, published.

Royal Designers for Industry appointed: Lucienne Day, David Mellor.

RSA Bicentenary medal awarded to Robin Darwin.

SIA Design Medal awarded to Pier Luigi Lervi

Duke's Prize for Elegant Design awarded by Sir Kenneth Clark, Sir Trenchard Cox, Lucienne Day and Jane Drew to Nicholas Sekers for furnishing fabrics made by West Cumberland Silk Mills.

Design Centre Awards selected by Martin Moss, Stefan Buzas, Elsbeth Juda, David Queensberry, Brian Shackel and Nigel Walters:

> BR heavy duty settee—designer, Robin Day; maker, Hille.
>
> Stainless steel dishes—designer, Robert Welch; maker, Old Hall.
>
> Pick-up arm—designers, A. Robertson-Aikman and W. J. Watkinson; maker, SME.
>
> Hoe and rake—designer, Brian Asquith; maker, Spear and Jackson.
>
> Dimex ceramic tiles—designer, Michael Caddy; maker, Wade.
>
> Trifoliate wallpaper—designer, Cliff Holden; maker, The Wall Paper Manufacturers.
>
> Sunflower printed cotton—designer, Howard Carter; maker, Heal Fabrics.
>
> Symbol cutlery and flatware—designer, David Mellor; maker, Walker & Hall.
>
> Vacco de luxe vacuum flask—designer, L. Leslie-Smith; maker, Vacco.
>
> Cawdor woven linen fabric—designers, staff and Peter M. Simpson; maker, Donald Brothers.

1963 Report on Engineering Design produced by committee appointed by Department of Scientific and Industrial Research, Chairman G. B. R. Feilden, to consider the present standing of mechanical engineering design.

London Transport Design Panel formed.

Systematic method for designers by L. Bruce Archer published.

Royal Designers for Industry appointed: Tom Eckersley, Robert Heritage.

RSA Bicentenary Medal awarded to Paul Reilly.

SIA Design Medal awarded to Ernest Race.

Duke's Prize for Elegant Design awarded by Sir Trenchard Cox, Lucienne Day, The Viscountess Eccles and David Hicks to Kenneth Grange for the Milward Courier Cordless electric shaver made by Henry Milward.

Design Centre Awards selected by O. B. Miller, Elgin Anderson, Trevor Dannatt, Natasha Kroll, David Mellor and Eirlys Roberts.

Pay-on-answer coin box—designers (engineering), Associated Automation with GPO, (case) Douglas Scott; maker, Associated Automation.

Harrington screen-printed cotton—designer, Humphrey Spender; maker, Cepea.

Heritage range of wall storage units—designer, Robert Heritage; maker, Archie Shine.

Trays and sectional hors d'oeuvre dishes (in grey translucent plastics)—designer, Noel Lefebvre; maker, Xlon.

Linking/stacking chair—designer, Clive Bacon; maker, Design Furnishing Contracts.

Lightweight slide storage box—designer, Albert Cragg; maker, Boots.

Cruachan screen printed cotton—designer, Peter McCulloch; maker, Hull Traders.

Corinthian inset fire unit—designer, David Brunton; maker, Belling.

Sheppey settees and chair—designer, Ernest Race; maker, Race.

Sola wash basin—designer, E. Stanley Ellis; maker, Twyfords.

Oregon dining chair—designer, Robert Heritage; maker, Archie Shine.

1964 House of Lords debate on industrial design: Lord Peddie rose to draw attention to the Annual Report of the CoID and 'to stress the importance of encouraging original design as a factor in the stimulation of exports and the improvement of home standards'.

First report of Summerson Council for Diplomas in Art and Design published.

Third report of Coldstream Council, on Post-Diploma Studies in Art and Design, published.

Terence Conran opened first Habitat household shop in Fulham Road.

Hornsey Mobile Caravan, designed by staff/student team under Clive Latimer, won Grand Prix at Milan Triennale.

Ernest Race died.

Royal Designers for Industry appointed: Hardy Amies, Alan Irvine, Alec Issigonis.

RSA Bicentenary Medal awarded to Anthony Heal.

SIA Design Medal awarded to Edward Bawden.

First Royal Society of Arts Presidential Awards for Design

Management made to Heal's, Conran, Hille, London Transport, Gilbey, Jaeger.

Duke's Prize for Elegant Design awarded by The Viscountess Eccles, Lucienne Day, Sir Trenchard Cox and David Hicks to David Queensberry for cut crystal glassware made by Webb Corbett.

Design Centre Awards selected by A. E. Everett Jones, Audrey Levy, Neville Ward, Katharine Whitehorn and George Williams:

Friedland 972 bell kit—designers, staff with Norman Stevenson; makers, V. & E. Friedland.

Moulton bicycle—designer, Alex Moulton; maker, Moulton Bicycles.

Brompton chair—designer, Ronald Carter; maker, Dancer & Hearne.

Nubian laminate—designer, Helen Dalby; maker, Formica.

Glendale woven fabric—designers, William Robertson and Peter Simpson; maker, Donald Bros.

Memory master clock—designer, staff and Robert Heritage; maker, English Clock Systems.

Brownie Vecta camera—designer, Kodak in consultation with Kenneth Grange; maker, Kodak.

Palladio Lamina wallpaper—designer, Deryck Healey; maker, The Wall Paper Manufacturers.

Insulated tumbler—designer, H. D. F. Creighton; maker, Insulex.

Garden shears—designers, staff and Hulme Chadwick; maker, Wilkinson Sword.

Printed fabrics, Shape Sixty-three and Division—designer, Shirley Craven; maker, Hull Traders.

Merlin electric clock—designers, staff and Robert Welch; maker, Westclox.

1965   Society of Industrial Artists renamed Society of Industrial Artists and Designers.

Report on Industrial and Engineering Design produced by working party of Federation of British Industries under G. B. R. Feilden.

Royal Designers for Industry appointed: Herbert Spencer, Robert Welch.

RSA Bicentenary Medal awarded to Hans Juda.

SIA Design Medal awarded to Misha Black.

Duke's Prize for Elegant Design awarded by The Viscountess Eccles, David Hicks, Ernestine Carter and Milner Gray to Peter Dickinson for auditorium seating by Race.

Design Centre Awards selected by Anthony Heal, Helen Challen, Shirley Conran, Robert Gutmann, Richard Stevens:

'Meridian One' Sanitary Suite—designers, Knud Holscher and Alan Tye with Alan H. Adams; maker, Adamsez.

'Arrowslim' fluorescent light fittings—designers, Peter Rodd and John Barnes; maker, Atlas.

'Gaylec' convector heater—designer, Bernard Burns; maker, Carnscot.

Cotton Satin 'Legend' 0700—designer, Alan Reynolds; maker, Edinburgh Weavers.

Yard Arm Pick-up Stick—designer, D. A. Morton; maker, Mabar.

'Embassy' Sterling Silver—designer and maker, David Mellor.

'Alveston' cutlery—designer, Robert Welch; maker, Old Hall.

Hille Wall Storage System—designers, Alan Turville and John Lewak; maker, Hille.

Rag Dolls—designers, Joy and Malcolm Wilcox; maker, Sari.

Plastics Handled Saw—designer, Brian Asquith; maker, Spear & Jackson.

Thornton Pic Slide Rules—designer, Norman Stevenson with staff; maker, Thornton.

'Kistna' furnishing fabric—designer, Sir Nicholas Sekers; maker, West Cumberland Silk Mills.

Hille Polypropylene Stacking Chair—designer, Robin Day; maker, Hille.

Ceiling Roses and Switches—designer, London & Upjohn; maker, GEC.

Hospital Wall Light—designer, Roger Brockbank; maker, Atlas.

Students' Striped Bedspreads—designers, H. W. Rothschild and Primavera Design Group; maker, Primavera.

1966   Plans first announced for combined London headquarters of Institute of Contemporary Arts, The Society of Industrial Artists, the Institute of Landscape Architects and the Designers and Art Directors' Association in Nash House Terrace, London.

Diplomas in Art and Design, equivalent to a first degree, first awarded to students completing courses at Colleges of Art.

Report 'A Plan for Polytechnics and Other Colleges', published by Department of Education and Science, proposing that many of the largest British Art Schools should be incorporated in local Polytechnics.

Engineering Design Centre established at Loughborough University.

Leverhulme Trust gave first travelling scholarships in industrial design.

George Williams, Director of Design, British Railways, died.

Royal Designer for Industry appointed: Natasha Kroll.

RSA Bicentenary medal awarded to Graham Hughes.

SIAD Design Medal awarded to Mary Quant.

Duke's Prize for Elegant Design awarded by Ernestine Carter, Mary Ward, Sir Colin Anderson and Milner Gray to Andrew Grima for jewellery.

Design Centre Awards selected by Sir Duncan Oppenheim, The

Hon. G. C. H. Chubb, Elsbeth Juda, Leslie Julius, Michael Laird, Leonard Manasseh:

'Automatic 1501' washing machine—designer, staff with Industrial Design Unit; maker, AEI–Hotpoint.

'Modric' architectural ironmongery—designers, Knud Holscher and Alan Tye; maker, G. & S. Allgood.

Desk Lamp 'Cantilever 41555'—designer, Gerald Abramovitz; maker, Best and Lloyd.

Hamilton stoneware—designers, Tarquin Cole and John Minshaw; maker, Govancroft.

Thrift Cutlery—designer, David Mellor; commissioned by Ministry of Public Building and Works.

1108 and 1111 Radios—designer, Robin Day with Douglas Jones; maker, Pye.

Flexible Chair—designer, Nicholas Frewing; maker, Race.

Quartet Major Lighting—designer, Robert Heritage; maker, Rotaflex.

Credaplan Individual Quick-Discs hotplates—designer, staff; maker, Simplex Electric.

STC Deltaphone and Deltaline Telephones—designer, Martyn Rowlands; maker, Standard Telephones and Cables.

Barbican hand rinse basin—designer, Chamberlin, Powell and Bon with staff; maker, Twyfords.

1967   Royal College of Art given University status (as a result of Robbins report on Higher Education, 1963).

Design Centre Awards renamed Council of Industrial Design Awards and scope broadened to include engineering design.

Crofton Gane died.

RSA Bicentenary Medal awarded to Harold Glover.

SIAD Design Medal awarded to Charles Eames.

RSA Presidential Awards for Design Management made to BTR Industries, Sainsbury, Clydesdale Bank, A. G. Thornton.

Duke's Prize for Elegant Design awarded by Sir Colin Anderson, Ernestine Carter, Milner Gray and Mary Ward to R. David Carter for 'Gas-Flo' system of points and fittings developed by Wales Gas Board.

CoID Design Awards—Consumer Goods Section—selected by Jasper Grinling, Brian Asquith, Rosamind Julius, Alan Irvine, Fiona MacCarthy:

'Iced Diamond' Refrigerators by Hotpoint

Ilfoprint Processors by Ilford

'PU Work Station' Office Furniture by Interiors International

Graphic System for Directional Road Signs commissioned by Ministry of Transport

'International' Range of Electric Convector Radiators by Morphy-Richards

'Tempest' Yacht by Richardson Boats and Plastics.

CoID Design Awards—Capital Goods Section—selected by W. L.

Mather, Professor Misha Black, H. G. Conway, Professor W. F. Floyd, C. H. Flurscheim, H. R. Heap, Jack Howe, D. B. Welbourn:

> Mascot 1600 Centre Lathe by Colchester Lathe Company
> Co-ordinate Inspection Machine by Ferranti
> Thompson-Watts Map Plotter by Hilger & Watts
> 1900 Series Computer by International Computers and Tabulators
> Power Rammer by Pegson
> Gas Cylinder by Reynolds Tube Company
> Hy-Mac Excavator by Rhymney Engineering for Peter Hamilton Equipment.

1968   Working party set up by Institute of Mechanical Engineers, at the request of the Council of Engineering Institutions, submitted report to Ministry of Technology advocating a single design council to promote design across the whole span of British industry.

Joint Coldstream/Summerson Committee of Inquiry into structure of art and design education prompted by student disturbances at Horney, Guildford and other colleges of art.

Stedjelich Museum, Amsterdam, held international exhibition of industrial design: Britain represented by Robin Day, Kenneth Grange, David Mellor and Robert Welch.

Paul Reilly knighted.

RSA Bicentenary medal awarded to Marcus Brumwell.

SIAD Design Medal awarded to Thomas Maldonado.

Duke's Prize for Elegant Design awarded by Sir Colin Anderson, The Marchioness of Anglesey, Robert Heritage and Mary Ward to David H. Powell for 'Nova' plastics tableware by Ecko.

CoID Awards—Consumer Goods—selected by Peter Tennant, Kathleen Darby, Althea McNeish, Geoffrey Salmon, Alan Tye:

> 'Clamcleat' rope cleats by Clamcleats
> Furnishing fabrics 'Chevron', 'Complex' and 'Extension' by Heal Fabrics
> Kompas 1 table by Hille
> Furnishing fabrics 'Simple Solar' and 'Five' by Hull Traders
> 'Trilateral' poster display unit by London and Provincial Poster Group
> 'Trimline' light by Merchant Adventurers
> 'Those Things' children's furniture by Perspective Designs
> 'Reigate' rocking chair by William Plunkett
> 'Coulsdon' coffee table by William Plunkett
> 'Silverspan' flourescent light fittings by Rotaflex
> 'Sealmaster' door and window seals by Sealmaster
> 'International' kitchen units by Wrighton.

CoID Awards—Capitals Goods—selected by A. R. Miller, F. C. Ashford, J. Atherton, Professor D. H. Chaddock, H. R. Heap, C. C. Mitchell, Professor W. T. Singleton, E. G. M. Wilkes:

'Hainsworth' worm gear reducer by J. H. Fenner
Flameproof motors by Mather and Platt
Colour television camera Mark VII by Marconi
'Sentinel' diesel hydraulic shunting locomotive by Rolls-Royce
'Crimpspin' CS12-600 false twist crimping machine by Ernest Scragg
'DD2' dockside crane by Stothert and Pitt.

1969   Proposals pressed forward for National Design Council, incorporating Council of Industrial Design, to cover engineering design as well as industrial design.

International Council for Societies of Industrial Design (ICSID) held conference in London.

SIA and DIA (with Institute of Contemporary Arts, Institute of Landscape Architects and Designers and Art Directors' Association) moved into headquarters in Nash House Terrace.

QE2 launched by Cunard, joint design co-ordinators James Gardner and Dennis Lennon.

Walter Gropius died.

Royal Designers for Industry appointed: Kenneth Grange, Mary Quant, Margaret Leischner, Ian Proctor.

RSA Bicentenary Medal awarded to Sir Duncan Oppenheim.

SIAD Design Medal awarded to Willy de Majo.

Duke's Prize for Elegant Design awarded by the Marchioness of Anglesey, Robin Day, Robert Heritage and Mary Quant to Jack Howe for cash dispenser MD2 by Chubb.

CoID Design Awards—Consumer Goods—selected by F. E. Shrosbree, Inette Austin-Smith, Gontran Goulden, Martin Grierson, Gilian Packard:

    Audio equipment by The Acoustical Manufacturing Company,
    'Superjet' 4448 reading light by Concord Lighting
    'Ease-e-load' trolleys by Deavin-Irvine
    Bollard light by Frederick Thomas
    Furnishing fabrics 'Polychrome', 'Concentric' and 'Mitre' by Heal Fabrics
    'Vinyl' wall coverings 'Gemini', 'Solitaire' and 'Tempo' by ICI
    'Kangol Reflex' car safety belt by Kangol
    Upholstery fabrics 'Spruce', 'Larch', 'Rowan' and 'Aspen' made by Margo
    'Big Screen' exhibition and display units by Marler Haley,
    'QE2' chair by Race
    'Roanrail 2' curtain track by Roanoid
    'Mercury 33' automatic deadlock by Yale.

CoID Design Awards—Capital Goods—selected by Matthew Wylie, Professor D. H. Chaddock, Dr R. Conrad, Ewen M'Ewen, Frank Height, B. G. L. Jackman, Noel London, C. C. Mitchell:

    Ceramic collar insulator by British Insulated Callenders & Cables
    'Monobox' overhead travelling crane by J. H. Carruthers

'Kaldo' steel furnace made by Ashmore, Benson, Pease
'K Major' diesel engine by Mirrlees National
'Vision Comparascope' by Vision Engineering
Knitting machine by Wildt Mellor Bromley.

1970　Joint Coldstream/Summerson Committee of Inquiry into structure of art and design education recommended replacement of vocational courses by new design technician's course.

Government decision 'not to proceed to set up the new Design Council in present circumstances' interpreted by optimists as a postponement, not a cancellation.

Association for Design Education formed to promote design in general education.

Experimental G.C.E. 'A' Level design syllabus introduced in Leicestershire schools.

Institute for Consumer Ergonomics jointly sponsored by Consumers Association and Loughborough University of Technology.

100 millionth Design Centre label produced for display on product selected for Design Index.

Exhibition of Modern Chairs at Whitechapel Gallery.

Royal Designers for Industry appointed: David Gentleman, G. Allan Hutt.

R.S.A. Bicentenary Medal awarded to T. C. H. Worthington.

Duke's Prize for Elegant Design awarded by the Marchioness of Anglesey, Mary Quant, Robert Heritage and Robin Day to Patrick Rylands for Trendon Toys.

CoID Design Awards—Consumer Goods—selected by Terence Conran, Alex Gordon, John Vaughan, Juliet Glynn Smith, Kenneth Grange:

> 'Opella 500' bath tap by I.M.I. Developments
> 'Star' mobile radiophone by Standard Telephones and Cables
> 'Apollo' lamp by J. R. M. Design
> Knockdown storage unit by Kewlox
> Disposable plastic cutlery by Ecko
> Dining table and chair by Plush Kicker
> 'Savannah' heating unit by Redfyre
> 'Hedway' sign by Syncronol
> 'Muraweave' jute wallcoverings by Boyle
> Range of hand-printed wallpapers by Osborne & Little
> 'Hebridean' upholstery fabrics by Donald Brothers
> 'Spiral' and 'Automation' furnishing fabrics by Heal Fabrics
> 'Hexagon' Brussels carpets by John Crossley.

CoID Design Awards—Capital Goods—selected by G. B. R. Feilden, Frank Height, Sir Arnold Lindley, Richard Stevens, S. H. Grylls, Dr. R. Conrad:

> 'Boss Mark III' range of forklift trucks by Lancer Boss
> Weighing machine TP30 by L. Oertling
> 'Autotest' system by Marconi Instruments
> 'Dualform Model 4E' press by Press & Shear Machinery Co.

The McArthur microscope made for Dr. John McArthur
'Wee Chieftain Mark 3' boiler by John Thompson Cochran
Additions to '1900' range of computers by International Computers
Container transporter crane by Stothert & Pitt.

1971   Arne Jacobsen died.

Royal Designers for Industry appointed: Gerald Benney, Ronald Carter, Jocelyn Herbert, Richard Levin, Neville Ward.

Duke's Prize for Elegant Design awarded by Robin Day, Peter Shepheard, Mary Quant and Lady Windlesham to Derek Power for atomic physics teaching apparatus by Teltron.

CoID Design Awards—Consumer Goods—selected by Leslie Julius, Joanne Brogden, Peter Glynn Smith, Derek Phillips and Norman Stevenson:

'Impregnable' padlocks by Ingersoll

'Avenger 16' power boat by Avenger Boat Co.

'Mariner' battery-powered clock by Taylor Instruments

'Globoots' children's boots by Globoot Footwear

Preview screen by Boots

Photographic darkroom equipment by Paterson Products

Pedestrian bridge by Butterly Engineering

'Powerflood' floodlamp by Concord Lighting.

CoID Design Awards—Capital Goods—selected by Dr. Alexander Moulton, David Carter, D. Downs, S. H. Grylls, Professor Brian Shackel, Richard Stevens, D. T. N. Williamson:

Automatic draughting system by Ferranti

Grinding machine by Churchill

'Spate' pump by William R. Selwood

Tensile testing instrument by Instron

Unican spectrophotometers by Pye Unican

'M41 Photoplan' research microscope by Vickers.

Book List

This reference list consists primarily of books about industrial design in Britain. Books about developments abroad are included only in so far as they are relevant to what was (or what was not) happening in Britain at the time.

ABBATT, L. (ed)   *The Stanley Book of Designs for Making Your Own Furniture*, 1966.

ADBURGHAM, Alison   *Shops and Shopping*, 1964.

AMAYA, Mario   *Art Nouveau*, 1966.

AMES, Winslow   *Prince Albert and Victorian Tastes*, 1967

ARCHER, L. Bruce   *Systematic method for designers*, 1965.

ARCHER, Michael   'Pre-Raphaelite Painted Furniture', *Country Life*, 1 April 1965.

ARNOT, R. Page   *William Morris, the Man and the Myth*, 1964.

ASHBEE, C. R.   *A Few Chapters on Workshop Reconstruction and Citizenship*, 1894; *An Endeavour towards the Teaching of John Ruskin and William Morris*, 1901; *Craftsmanship in Competitive Industry*, 1908.

ASHFORD, F. C.   *Designing for Industry—Some Aspects of the Product Designer's Work*, 1955.

ASLIN, Elizabeth   *The Aesthetic Movement*, 1969

BANHAM, Rayner   *Theory and Design in the First Machine Age*, 1960.

BATTERSBY, Martin   *The Decorative Twenties*, 1970.

BAYNES, Ken   *Industrial Design and the Community*, 1967; (ed) *Attitudes in Design Education*, 1969.

'Bauhaus, 50 years', Catalogue of Exhibition at Royal Academy, 1968.

BEARD, Geoffrey   *Modern Glass*, 1968.

BELL, Quentin   *The Schools of Design*, 1963.

BEMROSE, Geoffrey   *19th-Century English Pottery and Porcelain*, 1952.

BERESFORD-EVANS, J.   *Form in Engineering Design*, 1954.

BERTRAM, Anthony   *Design in Daily Life*, 1938.

BIRKS, Tony   *The Art of the Modern Potter*, 1967.

BLACK, Professor Misha   Cantor Lectures on Training of Industrial Designers for the Engineering Industries, *RSA Journal*, 1965.

BLAKE, John and Avril   *The Practical Idealists, a History of Design Research Unit*, 1969.

BOE, Alf   *From Gothic Revival to Functional Form*, 1954.

BRIGGS, Asa (ed)   *William Morris, Selected Writings and Designs*, 1962.

'British Art in Industry', illustrated catalogue of exhibition at Burlington House, 1935.

'Britain Can Make It', illustrated catalogue of CoID exhibition, Victoria and Albert Museum, 1946.

CAPLAN, David and Stewart G.   *British Trademarks and Symbols*, 1966.

CARRINGTON, Noel   *Design in the Home*, 1933; *Design and a Changing Civilization*, 1935; *The Shape of Things*, 1939; *Design in Civilization*, 1947; *Design and Decoration in the Home*, 1952.

CARRINGTON, Noel and HARRIS, Muriel (eds)   *British Achievement in Design*, 1946.

CASSON, Michael   *Pottery in Britain Today*, 1967.

CHAPMAN, Nigel   *Heating*, 1967.

CLARK, Sir Kenneth   *The Gothic Revival*, 1928.

COLE, Sir Henry   *Fifty Years of Public Work*, 1884.

CRANE, Walter   *The Claims of Decorative Art*, 1892; *An Artist's Reminiscences*, 1907; *William Morris to Whistler, Papers on Arts and Crafts and the Commonwealth*, 1911.

DAY, Lewis   *Everyday Art: Short Essays on the Arts Not-Fine*, 1882; *Nature and Ornament*, 1929.

Design Centre Book I, published by Council of Industrial Design, 1961.

Design Centre Book II, published by Council of Industrial Design, 1962.

Designers in Britain, illustrated review of SIA members' work, 1947, 1949, 1951, 1954, 1957, 1964.

DOREN, Harold Van   *Industrial Design (A Practical Guide)*, 1940

DOWLING, H. G.   *A Survey of British Industrial Arts*, 1935.

EASTLAKE, Charles L.   *Hints on Household Tastes in Furniture*, 1868.

EDWARDS, Ralph and RAMSEY, L. G. G. (eds)   *Early Victorian (1830–1860) Connoisseur Period Guide*, 1958.

FARR, Michael   *Design in British Industry—A Mid-Century Survey*, 1955; *Design Management*, 1966.

'Festival of Britain', Illustrated catalogue, 1951. Souvenir booklet 'Design in the Festival', 1951. Souvenir book of Crystal Design (The Festival Pattern Group), 1951.

'Festival of Britain, The Story of', official report, 1951.

'Festival of Britain, Three Cantor Lectures on', by Sir Gerald Barry to RSA, reprinted in *Journal 4880*, August 22, 1952.

FLOUD, Peter   BBC talks on William Morris, reprinted in *The Listener*, October 7 and 14, 1954.

FRANKLIN, Colin   *The Private Presses*, 1969.

FRAYN, Michael   Account of 'The Festival of Britain' in *The Age of Austerity*, ed. Michael Sissons and Philip French, 1963.

GIBBS-SMITH, C. H.	*The Great Exhibition of 1851*, 1950.
GILL, Eric	*Autobiography*, 1945.
GILLIATT, Mary	*English Style*, 1967.
GLOAG, John	*Design in Modern Life*, 1934; *Industrial Art Explained*, 1934; *The Missing Technician in Industrial Production*, 1944; *English Tradition in Design*, 1947; *Good Design means Good Business*, 1947; *Self-training for Industrial Designers*, 1947; *Victorian Taste*, 1962; *The Englishman's Chairs*, 1964.
Goldsmiths, Worshipful Company of	*Modern Silver*, 1954; *Modern Silver, Review of Gold and Silver*, 1959; *Modern British Silver, Illustrated Review*, 1963; *Modern British Jewellery, Illustrated Review*, 1963.
GOSLETT, Dorothy	*Professional Practice for Designers*, 1961.
GOULDEN, Gontran	*Bathrooms*, 1966.
	Great Exhibition 1851. Illustrated Catalogue of, 1851.
	Great Exhibition 1851, Reports by the Juries, 1852.
GROPIUS, Walter	'Bauhaus': Paper given to DIA, reprinted *RIBA Journal*, May 19, 1934; *New Architecture and the Bauhaus*, 1935; *Design and Industry*, 1950.
HENDERSON, Philip	*William Morris, his Life, Work and Friends*, 1967.
HENRION, F. H. K. and PARKIN, Alan	*Design Co-ordination and Corporate Image*, 1967.
HILLIER, Bevis	*Art Deco*, 1968.
HIRSCHFELD-MACK, L.	*The Bauhaus*, 1963.
HOLME, Geoffrey	*Industrial Design and the Future*, 1934.
HOUGH, Graham	*The Last Romantics*, 1949.
HOWARTH, Thomas	*Charles Rennie Mackintosh and the Modern Movement*, 1952.
HUGHES, Graham	*Modern Jewellery, 1890–1963*, 1963. *Modern Silver, 1880–1967*, 1967.
HUGHES-STANTON, Corin	*Transport Design*, 1968.
	International Exhibition of 1862, illustrated booklet of exhibits issued in conjunction with 'London 1862' exhibition at Victoria and Albert Museum, 1962
JAFFE, H. L. C.	*De Stijl*, 1956.
JARVIS, A.	*Things We See—Indoors and Out*, 1946.
JOEL, David	*The Adventure of British Furniture*, 1953.
JOEL, David	*The British Furniture Revolution, 1851 to the Present Day*, 1970.
JONES, Prof. J. Christopher	*Design Methods*, 1970.
JONES, Owen	*Grammar of Ornament*, 1856.
KLEIN, Bernat	*Eye for Colour*, 1965.
LARKIN, Brian	*Metalwork Designs of Today*, 1969.
LAVER, James	*The Liberty Story*, 1959.
LEACH, Bernard	*A Potter's Work*, 1967.
LETHABY, W. R.	*Philip Webb and his Work*, 1935. *Form in Civilization, Papers on Art and Labour*, 1957.
LETHABY, W. R. and others	*Ernest Gimson, his Life and Work*, 1924.
LOEWY, Raymond	*Never Leave Well Enough Alone*, 1951.
LOUDON, John C.	*Encyclopedia of Cottage, Farm and Villa Architecture and Furniture*, 1833.

MACKAIL, J. W.   *Life of William Morris*, 1899.

'Mackintosh, Charles Rennie: Furniture', illustrated catalogue of Glasgow School of Art Collection, 1968.

'Mackintosh, Charles Rennie: Ironwork and Metalwork', Illustrated catalogue of Glasgow School of Art Collection, 1968.

'Mackintosh, Charles Rennie: Architecture, Design, Painting', catalogue to Centenary Exhibition at Royal Scottish Museum and Victoria and Albert Museum, 1968.

MACLEOD, Robert   *Charles Rennie Mackintosh*, 1968.

MADSEN, S. T.   *The Sources of Art Nouveau*, 1952.

MARTIN, J. L. and SPEIGHT, S.   *The Flat Book*, 1939.

MAYALL, W. H.   *Industrial Design for Engineers*, 1967; *Machines and Perception in Industrial Design*, 1968.

MEADE, Dorothy   *Bedrooms*, 1967.

MIDDLETON, Michael   *Group Practice in Design*, 1967.

MOODY, Ella   *Modern Furniture*, 1966.

MORRIS, May   *William Morris, Artist, Writer, Socialist*, 1936.

MORRIS, William   *Collected Works*, 1910–15.

Morris, William, Illustrated Booklet of Designs, Victoria and Albert Museum, 1958.

'Morris & Company 1861–1940', Catalogue of Commemorative Exhibition, Arts Council, 1961.

'Morris, William, The Work Of', Catalogue of Exhibition at The Times Bookshop, by William Morris Society, 1962.

NAYLOR, Gillian   *The Bauhaus*, 1968.

PEVSNER, Nikolaus   *Pioneers of the Modern Movement*, 1936, revised version, *Pioneers of Modern Design*, published Penguin, 1960; *An Enquiry into Industrial Art in England*, 1937; *Academies of Art*, 1940; *High Victorian Design*, 1951; *The Englishness of English Art*, expanded version of Reith Lectures broadcast in 1955, 1956; *The Sources of Modern Architecture and Design*, 1968; *Studies in Art, Architecture and Design*, 1968.

PHILLIPS, Derek   *Lighting*, 1966.

PILDITCH, James and SCOTT, Douglas   *The Business of Product Design*, 1965.

PRIZEMAN, John   *Kitchens*, 1966.

PUGIN, A. W. N.   *Gothic Furniture*, 1835; *Contrasts*, 1836; *The True Principles of Pointed or Christian Architecture*, 1841.

PYE, David   *Nature of Design*, 1964.

RAYNER, Claire   *For Children*, 1967.

READ, Sir Herbert   *Art and Industry*, 1934.

READ, Sir Herbert (intr.)   *Practice of Design*, 1946.

REDGRAVE, Richard   *Report on the Present State of Design as Applied to Manufactures*, 1857.

ROGERS, J. C.   *Modern English Furniture*, 1930.

ROLT, L. T. C.   *Victorian Engineering*, 1970.

ROTHENSTEIN, Sir William   A Plea for a Wider Use of Artists and Craftsmen, lecture to Sheffield Technical School, 1916.

RUSKIN, John   *Seven Lamps of Architecture*, 1849; *Stones of Venice*, 1851–3.

RUSSELL, Sir Gordon — *Furniture* ('Things we See' Series), 1953; *Looking at Furniture*, 1964; *Designer's Trade*, 1968.

SALMON, Geoffrey — *Storage*, 1967.

SCHEIDIG, Walther — *Crafts of the Weimar Bauhaus*, 1967.

SCHMUTZLER, Robert — *Art Nouveau*, 1964.

SEDDING, John — *Art and Handicraft*, 1893.

SEIZ, P. and
CONSTANTINE, M. — *Art Nouveau—Art and Design at the Turn of the Century*, 1959.

SHARP, Peter — *Sound and Vision*, 1967.

SKELTON, Robin (ed) — *Herbert Read, a memorial symposium*, 1970.

SPEAIGHT, Robert — *The Life of Eric Gill*, 1966.

STENNETT-WILSON, R. — *The Beauty of Modern Glass*, 1958.

STEWART, Cecil — *Art in Adversity, A Short History of the Regional College of Art*, Manchester, 1953.

TEAGUE, Walter Dorwin — *Design This Day: The Technique of Order in the Machine Age*, 1940.

THOMPSON, Paul — *The Work of William Morris*, 1967.

VALLANCE, Aymer — *William Morris, His Art, Writings and Public Life*, 1909.

'Victorian and Edwardian Decorative Art', catalogue to Victoria and Albert Museum Exhibition, 1952.

'Victorian Furniture', illustrated booklet by Victoria and Albert Museum, 1962.

'The Visual Arts' report, sponsored by trustees of Dartington Hall, published by Political & Economic Planning and Oxford University Press, 1946.

WARD, Mary and Neville — *Living Rooms*, 1967.

WATKINSON, Ray — *William Morris as Designer*, 1967.

WINGLER, Hans M. — *The Bauhams*, 1969.

WYATT, M. D. — Report on the Furniture at the Paris Exhibition of 1855, 1856. Industrial Arts of the Nineteenth Century, at the Great Exhibition, 1851, 1851–3.

YOUNG, Dennis and Barbara — *Furniture in Britain Today*, 1964.

PERIODICALS

Architectural Review, 1897–   .

Ark, Journal of Royal College of Art.

Art and Design, Monthly bulletin of Central Institute of Art and Design, 1942–48.

Commercial Art and Industry, later *Art and Industry*, 1926–58.

Council of Industrial Design Annual Reports, 1944–   .

Design, published by Council of Industrial Design, 1949–   .

Design and Industries Journals, News Sheets and Year Books, 1918–   .

Design in Industry, published by DIA, 1932; replaced by *Design for Today*, published in association with DIA, 1933; later replaced by *Trend in Design of Everyday Things*, 1936.

House and Garden.

Ideal Home.

Journal of Design and Manufactures, 1849–52.

Royal Society of Arts Proceedings.

Society of Industrial Artists, newsheets and journals, later *The Designer*.

The Studio, later *Studio International*, 1893–   .

Acknowledgements

In preparing this book I have had a great deal of valuable assistance, including special facilities for visits, from manufacturers, retailers, schools of art and various public bodies and societies.

I should like to thank the following:

Paul and Marjorie Abbatt; Aram; Armitage Ware;

Beithcraft Furniture; Birmingham College of Art and Design; Bowman's; Briglin Pottery; Brinton's; Bristol Guild of Applied Art; British Motor Corporation; British Rail;

Caithness Glass; Camberwell School of Arts and Crafts; Carpet Manufacturing Co; Carpet Trades; Central School of Art and Design; Colston; Confederation of British Industry; Conran; Council of Industrial Design; Crafts Centre;

Dartington Glass; Design and Industries Association; Design Furnishing Contracts; Design Workshop; Donald Brothers; Dryad; Dunn's of Bromley; Charles Early;

Edinburgh College of Art; Edinburgh Weavers; Ercol;

Firth Carpets;

Glasgow School of Art; Goodearl; Govancroft; T. G. Green;

Heal's; High Wycombe College of Art and Technology; H. K. Furniture; Hoover; Hopewell's; Hornsey College of Art; Hygena; H. & R. Johnson;

Kingston College of Art; Kosset;

Leeds College of Art; Leicester College of Art; Liverpool College of Art; L. M. Furniture; London Transport;

Hugh MacKay; A. H. MacIntosh; Malkin; Manchester College of Art and Design; Merchant Adventurers; Metamec; Minty; Moorcroft; Morris of Glasgow; Moulton; Myers;

Nairn Linoleum; National Council for Diplomas in Art and Design;

Old Hall; O. M. K. Furniture;
Peerless Built-in Furniture; Perspective Designs; Pilkington Tiles; Poole Pottery; Pye;
Race; Ravensbourne College of Art and Design; Remploy; Reynolds Woodware; Richards Tiles; Guy Rogers; Royal Society of Arts; Royal Worcester; Rural Industries Bureau; Gordon Russell;
Sanderson; Sekers; Sheffield College of Art; Archie Shine; Slumberland; Smith's Clocks; Society of Industrial Artists and Designers; Stag; Stockwell; Stoddard; Stourbridge College of Art;
Tamesa; Tibor;
Victoria and Albert Museum; Viners;
Walker and Hall; Bernard Wardle; Webb Corbett; Wedgwood; Westclox; David Whitehead; Wolverhampton College of Art; Worshipful Company of Goldsmiths; Wrighton; Wylie & Lochhead.

I should like to thank the following people, all of whom I have either talked to or written to, and who have given me helpful information and ideas for this book:

Pat Albeck; Geoffrey Alpe; Sir Colin Anderson; Zeev Aram; Dr L. Bruce Archer; Tom Arnold; Brian Asquith; Frank Austin; H. Jefferson Barnes; John Barnes; Edward Barnsley; Edward Bawden; Gerald Benney; J. Beresford-Evans; Robert Best; Professor Misha Black; John Blake; Ronald Brookes; Paul Burall; Shirley Bury; Stefan Buzas;
Dugald Cameron; Robert Cantor; Noel Carrington; R. David Carter; Ronald Carter; Sir Hugh Casson; Hulme Chadwick; Tarquin Cole; Neville Conder; E. Cooke-Yarborough; James Cousins; Shirley Craven; Robin Cruikshank;
Helen Dalby; Sir Robin Darwin; Tarby Davenport; Robin Day; Ronald Dickens; Peter Dingley; Robert Dodd; John Donald; Geoffrey Dunn;
Brian Edwards;
Ronald Facius; Colleen Farr; Gillian Farr; Michael Farr; George Fejer; J. Findlater;
James Gardner; Alec Gardner-Medwin; John Gloag; Harold Glover; Professor Robert Goodden; Kenneth Grange; John Grant; Milner Gray; Roy Gray; Martin Grierson; Andrew Grima; Frank Guille;
Geoffrey Harcourt; Claude Hart; Colin Haxby; Christopher Heal; Adrian Heath; Frank Height; F. H. K. Henrion; Robert Heritage; Peter Heyward; Oliver Hill; the late Oliver Hill; Jack Hilton; Kenneth Holmes; Felix Holtom; Ronald Homes; Jack Howe; Kenneth Howes; Miriam Howitt; Derek Hudson; Corin Hughes-Stanton; Richard Huws;
Peter Inchbald; Ronald Ingles; Alan Irvine;

Dan Johnston; J. W. Noel Jordan; Elspeth Juda; Rosamind Julius;

Tom Karen; R. M. Kay; Bernat Klein; Peter Kneebone;

Clive Latimer; Howell Leadbeater; the late Margaret Leischner; S. C. Leslie; Richard Levin; Audrey Levy; Ian Logan; Noel London; W. M. de Majo; Eric Marshall; Enid Marx; Alister Maynard; Peter McCulloch; Raymond McGrath; Professor Andrew McLaren Young; David Medd; John Mellor; Peter Metcalfe; Sir Francis Meynell; Sir Bernard Miller; John Moon; Martin Moss, Keith Murray;

Neville Neal; Evelyn New; S. H. Nichols; James Noel-White; the late Harry Norris;

Eric Pamphilon; Geoffrey Peach; James Pilditch; William Plunkett; Diana Pollock; Edward Pond; T. E. Preston; Jack Pritchard; Jack Proctor; Patrick Purcell; David Pye;

The Marquis of Queensberry;

A. B. Read; Tibor Reich; Sir Paul Reilly; Martyn Rowlands; Sir Gordon Russell; R. D. Russell;

Norah Schlegel; Gaby Schreiber; Douglas Scott; Cecilia Lady Sempill; Herbert Simon; George Sneed; The Earl of Snowdon; Humphrey Spender; Jack Stafford; R. Stennett-Wilson; Richard Stevens; Norman Stevenson; Robert Stewart; Frank Stockwell; Marianne Straub;

John Tandy; Mirjana Teofanovic; Donald Tomlinson; Cycill Tomrley; Michael Tree; Alan Tye; Keith Tyssen;

Howard Upjohn;

Peter Wall; Nigel Walters; C. Leslie Ward; Neville Ward; John Waterer; John Webb; Robert Welch; David White; E. G. M. Wilkes.

I should also like to thank Mrs and the late Mr Colin Mellor, Mrs G. W. Parsisson and Mrs Sandra Pascoe who have assisted in many different ways.

Sources of Illustrations in Text

CHAPTER ONE

1   Henry Cole teapot, *Victoria and Albert Museum*.
2   Christopher Dresser pitcher and glasses, *Victoria and Albert Museum*.
3   Edward William Godwin table, *City Art Gallery, Bristol*.
4   Henry Cole teaset, *Victoria and Albert Museum*.
5   Edward William Godwin chair, *Victoria and Albert Museum*.
6   William Burges cabinet, *Victoria and Albert Museum*.
7   Christopher Dresser teapot, *James Dixon, Sheffield*.
8   Bruce J. Talbert fabric, *Victoria and Albert Museum*.
9   Christopher Dresser glassware, *Victoria and Albert Museum*.
10 Owen Jones fabric, *Victoria and Albert Museum*.
11 Richard Redgrave decanter, *Victoria and Albert Museum*.
12 William Burges (?) bookcase, *Christie's, London*.
13 Edward William Godwin table, *City Art Gallery, Bristol*.
14 Edward William Godwin sideboard, *Victoria and Albert Museum*.
15 Owen Jones fabric, *Victoria and Albert Museum*.
16 Owen Jones fabric, *Victoria and Albert Museum*.
17 Alfred Stevens door-knocker, *Victoria and Albert Museum*.
18 Bruce J. Talbert fabric, *Victoria and Albert Museum*.

CHAPTER TWO

19 Ambrose Heal cupboard, *Heal and Son*.
20 Ambrose Heal wardrobe, *Heal and Son*.
21 Ambrose Heal sideboard, *Heal and Son*.
22 Ambrose Heal wardrobe, *Heal and Son*.
23 Ernest Gimson cabinet, *Leicester Museum*.
24 Sidney Barnsley cabinet, *Edward Barnsley*.
25 Ernest Gimson interior, Daneway House, *Country Life*.
26 Ernest Gimson table, *Leicester Museum*.

27 Ernest Gimson chair, *Victoria and Albert Museum.*

28 Ernest Gimson firedog, *Leicester Museum.*

29 Charles Rennie Mackintosh cutlery, *T. and R. Annan, Glasgow.*

30 Charles Rennie Mackintosh chair, *Photograph, Keith Gibson; Paul Hamlyn.*

31 Charles Rennie Mackintosh fish knife and fork, *Museum of Modern Art, New York.*

32 Charles Rennie Mackintosh interior, Hill House, *Photograph, Keith Gibson; Paul Hamlyn.*

33 Charles Rennie Mackintosh chair, *Victoria and Albert Museum.*

34 Charles Rennie Mackintosh chairs, *Photograph, Keith Gibson; Paul Hamlyn.*

35 C. F. A. Voysey fabric, *Victoria and Albert Museum.*

36 C. F. A. Voysey fabric, *Victoria and Albert Museum.*

37 C. F. A. Voysey fabric, *Victoria and Albert Museum.*

38 C. F. A. Voysey teapot, *Victoria and Albert Museum.*

39 C. F. A. Voysey writing desk, *Victoria and Albert Museum.*

40 Philip Webb chimney-piece, *National Monuments Record.*

41 Philip Webb and William Morris interior, Red House, *Country Life.*

42 R. Norman Shaw (?) chair, *Victoria and Albert Museum.*

43 William Morris chair, *Victoria and Albert Museum.*

44 Edward Burne-Jones piano, *Victoria and Albert Museum.*

45 William Morris embroidered panel, *Victoria and Albert Museum.*

46 William Morris fabric, *Victoria and Albert Museum.*

47 William Morris fabric, *Victoria and Albert Museum.*

48 William Morris wallpaper, *Victoria and Albert Museum.*

49 A. H. Mackmurdo writing desk, *William Morris Gallery, Walthamstow.*

50 A. H. Mackmurdo chair, *William Morris Gallery, Walthamstow.*

51 A. H. Mackmurdo fabric, *Victoria and Albert Museum.*

52 E. G. Punnett chair, *Victoria and Albert Museum.*

53 Liberty and Co. stool, *Victoria and Albert Museum.*

54 Philip Webb glass, *Victoria and Albert Museum.*

55 M. H. Baillie Scott cabinet, *Victoria and Albert Museum.*

56 George Walton glass, *Victoria and Albert Museum.*

57 M. H. Baillie Scott seat, *Victoria and Albert Museum.*

58 C. R. Ashbee silver dish, *Victoria and Albert Museum.*

59 Della Robbia pottery vase, *Victoria and Albert Museum.*

60 C. R. Ashbee mustard pot, *Kunstgewerbemuseum, Zurich.*

61 William de Morgan dish, *Victoria and Albert Museum.*

62 W. A. S. Benson lamp, *Victoria and Albert Museum.*

63 W. R. Lethaby sideboard, *Victoria and Albert Museum.*

64 M. H. Baillie Scott clock, *Victoria and Albert Museum.*

65 Philip Webb table, *Victoria and Albert Museum.*

66 Arthur Silver candlesticks, *Victoria and Albert Museum.*

67 Arthur Dixon coffee jugs, *Victoria and Albert Museum.*

68 Archibald Knox jewel box, *Museum of Modern Art, New York.*

110   Serge Chermayeff chair, *B.B.C.*
111   Raymond McGrath interior, *Raymond McGrath.*
112   Raymond McGrath interior, *Raymond McGrath.*
113   Maxwell Fry and Jack Howe interior, *Heal and Son.*
114   Walter Gropius waste-paper basket, *Gordon Russell.*
115   Brian O'Rorke interior, *P. & O.*
116   Brian O'Rorke interior, *P. & O.*
117   Dorland Hall exhibition entrance, *Architectural Review.*
118   Dorland Hall exhibition dining room, *Architectural Review.*
119   London Transport bus shelter, *London Transport Board.*
120   London Transport Underground booking hall, *London Transport Board.*
121   London Transport LT-type bus, *London Transport Board.*
122   London Transport trolleybus, *London Transport Board.*
123   London Transport Underground coach, *London Transport Board.*
124   Marion Dorn fabric, *London Transport Board.*
125   Marion Dorn fabric, *London Transport Board.*
126   Marion Dorn fabric, *London Transport Board.*
127   Marian Pepler rug, *R. D. Russell.*
128   Marian Pepler rug, *R. D. Russell.*
129   Paul Nash fabric, *Victoria and Albert Museum.*
130   Marianne Straub fabric, *Straub.*
131   Duncan Grant fabric, *Design and Industries Association.*
132   Duncan Grant fabric, *Victoria and Albert Museum.*
133   Keith Murray glass, *Victoria and Albert Museum.*
134   Keith Murray beer mugs, *Murray.*
135   Keith Murray cocktail set, *Murray.*
136   Keith Murray cocktail cups, *Murray.*
137   Eric Ravilious bowl, *Victoria and Albert Museum.*
138   Susie Cooper china, *Wedgwood.*
139   Joseph Bourne casseroles, *Victoria and Albert Museum.*
140   Eric Ravilious mugs, *Wedgwood.*
141   Milner Gray and Graham Sutherland china, *Design Research Unit.*
142   R. Y. Goodden glass bowl, *Goodden.*
143   R. Y. Goodden powder bowl, *Goodden.*
144   Graham Sutherland glassware, *Design Research Unit.*
145   Milner Gray silver bowl, *Design Research Unit.*
146   Milner Gray Ginger Jack bottle, *Design Research Unit.*
147   Milner Gray wine bottle, *Design Research Unit.*
148   Best and Lloyd 'Bestlite', *Best and Lloyd.*
149   A. B. Read light fitting, *Read.*
150   A. B. Read light fitting, *Read.*
151   E. S. Corner car, *Galt.*
152   John Waterer luggage, *Waterer.*
153   'Feed the Brute', *Design and Industries Association.*

CHAPTER FIVE

CHAPTER SIX

196 Booth and Ledeboer sideboard, *Gordon Russell.*

197 Ward and Austin bedroom furniture, *Photograph, Millar and Harris; Ward and Austin.*

198 Ward and Austin bedroom furniture, *Photograph, Dennis Hooker; Ward and Austin.*

199 Robin Day bed settee, *Photograph, Mann; Day.*

200 Robin Day seating, *Photograph, Mann; Day.*

201 Robert Heritage storage unit, *Heritage.*

202 Robin Day television, *Council of Industrial Design.*

203 Robert Heritage sideboard, *Council of Industrial Design.*

204 John and Sylvia Reid dining furniture, *Photograph, Pilkington Studios; Stag Cabinet Co.*

205 George Fejer and Eric Pamphilon furniture, *Gee Advertising.*

206 Marian Mahler fabric, *David Whitehead.*

207 Marian Mahler fabric, *David Whitehead.*

208 Jacqueline Groag fabric, *David Whitehead.*

209 Lucienne Day fabric, *Day.*

210 Lucienne Day linen, *Council of Industrial Design.*

211 Humphrey Spender fabric, *Council of Industrial Design.*

212 Tibor Reich fabric, *Tibor.*

213 Ronald Grierson carpet, *Photograph, George Miles; Stockwell.*

214 F. G. Hobden fabric, *Council of Industrial Design.*

215 Audrey Tanner carpet, *Foote, Cone and Belding.*

216 Susie Cooper pottery, *Wedgwood.*

217 Edward Bawden muffin dish, *Victoria and Albert Museum.*

218 Robert Stewart storage jars, *Council of Industrial Design.*

219 R. Stennett-Willson glass, *Council of Industrial Design.*

220 Milner Gray, Kenneth Lamble and John Cochrane glassware, *Photograph, John Maltby; Design Research Unit.*

221 Noel London and Howard Upjohn saucepans; *Council of Industrial Design.*

222 Robert Welch jugs, *Photograph, Dennis Hooker; Welch.*

223 Robert Welch silver, *Welch.*

224 David Mellor teaset, *Council of Industrial Design.*

225 Robert Welch toast rack, *Photograph, Dennis Hooker; Welch.*

226 David Mellor cutlery, *Photograph, Dennis Hooker; Mellor.*

227 E. Cooke-Yarborough and Ronald Homes light fitting, *Conelight.*

228 D. W. Morphy iron, *Morphy-Richards.*

229 G. W. F. Longman refrigerator, *Council of Industrial Design.*

230 Jacke Howe clock, *Howe.*

231 David Ogle fire, *Council of Industrial Design.*

232 R. David Carter castors, *Carter.*

233 John Waterer leather bag, *Photograph, Briggs; Waterer.*

234 Hulme Chadwick pruner, *Council of Industrial Design.*

235 London Transport bus stop, *London Transport.*

236 Richard Stevens lighting column, *Photograph, John Maltby; Stevens.*

237 Neville Conder telephone kiosk, *Council of Industrial Design.*

274 Lucienne Day carpet, *I. & C. Steele.*

275 Lucienne Day carpet, *I. & C. Steele.*

276 Mary Yonge carpet, *I. & C. Steele.*

277 Catherine Beevers carpet, *Andrew Gaskell.*

278 Catherine Beevers wallpaper, *The Wall Paper Manufacturers.*

279 Robert Welch cast-iron, *Welch.*

280 Tarquin Cole and John Minshaw casseroles, *Photograph, Jane Gate; Ceramic Consultants.*

281 Frank Thrower glass, *Dartington Glass.*

282 David Queensberry and Jessie Tait tableware, *Council of Industrial Design.*

283 Robert Welch candlesticks, *Welch.*

284 David Mellor teapot, *Council of Industrial Design.*

285 Robert Welch teapot, *Welch.*

286 David Mellor cutlery, *Photograph, Banks Turner; Mellor.*

287 Robert Welch condiment set, *Welch.*

288 David Mellor tea and coffee pots, *Photograph, Dennis Hooker; Mellor.*

289 Robert Welch clock, *Council of Industrial Design.*

290 D. M. R. Brunton fire, *Council of Industrial Design.*

291 Kenneth Grange camera, *Council of Industrial Design.*

292 Kenneth Grange shaver, *Council of Industrial Design.*

293 Robert Heritage light fittings, *Council of Industrial Design.*

294 Norman Stevenson bells, *Council of Industrial Design.*

295 Kenneth Grange iron, *Grange.*

296 Hulme Chadwick garden shears, *Council of Industrial Design.*

297 Joy and Malcolm Wilcox cut-out doll, *Council of Industrial Design.*

298 Martyn Rowlands telephone, *Council of Industrial Design.*

299 John Gould train, *Paul and Marjorie Abbatt.*

300 Noel London and Howard Upjohn microscope, *London and Upjohn.*

301 Noel London and Howard Upjohn computer installation, *Photograph, Peter Waugh; London and Upjohn.*

302 R. David Carter gas fitting, *Carter.*

303 David Mellor gear-measuring machine, *Council of Industrial Design.*

304 R.C.A. Research Unit hospital bed, *Royal College of Art.*

305 Mather and Platt flameproof motors, *Council of Industrial Design.*

306 David Mellor traffic signals, *Photograph, Dennis Hooker; Mellor.*

307 Jock Kinneir traffic sign, *Council of Industrial Design.*

308 Alex Moulton bicycle, *Moulton Bicycles.*

309 Alec Issigonis car, *British Motor Corporation.*

310 Douglas Scott Associates excavator, *Council of Industrial Design.*

311 Misha Black and James Williams aircraft, *Photograph, Cyril Peckham; Design Research Unit.*

312 Misha Black and J. Beresford-Evans electric locomotives, *Photograph, Sam Lambert; Design Research Unit.*

SOURCES OF ILLUSTRATIONS
USED AT CHAPTER OPENINGS

Chapter One — Great Exhibition closing ceremony, October 1851.
Victoria and Albert Museum.

Chapter Two — Philip Clisset chair bodger, portrait by Maxwell Balfour, 1898.
City Museum, Hereford.

Chapter Three — Harry H. Peach (1874–1936).
Geoffrey Peach

Chapter Four — London Transport bus stop signs, Knightsbridge, 1936.
London Transport.

Chapter Five — 'Britain Can Make It'
queues outside Victoria and Albert Museum, 1946.
Hulton Press.

Chapter Six — The Duke of Edinburgh with his Prize for Elegant Design 1959, the Prestcold 'Packaway' refrigerator.
Judges: left to right, Sir John Summerson, Sir Basil Spence, Audrey Withers, Lady Casson.
Council of Industrial Design.

Chapter Seven — Some of the 370 delegates to the International Design Congress, London 1966.
Council of Industrial Design.

Index

Bazaar, Bishop, Bowler, Bowman's, Boy and Girl, Brown's, Design Design, Dobbie, Dunbar Hay, Dunn's, Fortnum and Mason, Gane, Gear, Galt, Habitat, Hammonds, Harland, Harrods, Heals, Hopewell's, Interior Decorations, John for Toys, Jones, Lewis's, Liberty's, Morgan, Owl and Pussycat, Play and Learn, Primavera, Russell, Shape, Trend, Waring and Gillow, Woollands, York Tenn